# brilliant

## Microsoft®
# Access
## 2007

# POCKET BOOK

### S. E. Slack

PEARSON
Prentice
Hall

Harlow, England • London • New York • Boston • San Francisco • Toronto • Sydney • Singapore • Hong Kong
Tokyo • Seoul • Taipei • New Delhi • Cape Town • Madrid • Mexico City • Amsterdam • Munich • Paris • Milan

**Pearson Education Limited**
Edinburgh Gate
Harlow CM20 2JE
Tel: +44 (0) 1279 623623
Fax: +44 (0) 1279 431059
Website: www.pearsoned.co.uk

First published in Great Britain in 2007

ISBN: 978-0-132-05924-4

**British Library Cataloguing-in-Publication Data**
A catalogue record for this book is available from the British Library.

10 9 8 7 6 5 4 3 2 1
11 10 09 08 07

Typeset in 10pt Helvetica Roman by 30
Printed and bound in Great Britain by Ashford Colour Press Ltd, Gosport


*The Publisher's policy is to use paper manufactured from sustainable forests.*

# Brilliant Pocket Books

## What you need to know – when you need it!

When you're working on your PC and come up against a problem that you're unsure how to solve, or want to accomplish something in an application that you aren't sure how to do, where do you look? If you are fed up with wading through pages of background information in unwieldy manuals and training guides trying to find the piece of information or advice that you need RIGHT NOW, and if you find that helplines really aren't that helpful, then Brilliant Pocket Books are the answer!

Brilliant Pocket Books have been developed to allow you to find the info that you need easily and without fuss and to guide you through each task using a highly visual step-by-step approach – providing exactly what you need to know, when you need it!

Brilliant Pocket Books are concise, easy-to-access guides to all of the most common important and useful tasks in all of the applications in the Office 2007 suite. Short, concise lessons make it really easy to learn any particular feature, or master any task or problem that you will come across in day-to-day use of the applications.

**When you are faced with any task on your PC, whether major or minor, that you are unsure about, your Brilliant Pocket Book will provide you with the answer – almost before you know what the question is!**

# Brilliant Pocket Books Series

**Series Editor: Joli Ballew**

Brilliant Microsoft® Access 2007 Pocket Book  *S.E.Slack*

Brilliant Microsoft® Excel 2007 Pocket Book  *J. Peter Bruzzese*

Brilliant Microsoft® Office 2007 Pocket Book  *Jerri Ledford & Rebecca Freshour*

Brilliant Microsoft® Outlook 2007 Pocket Book  *Meryl K. Evans*

Brilliant Microsoft® PowerPoint 2007 Pocket Book  *S. E. Slack*

Brilliant Microsoft® Windows Vista 2007 Pocket Book  *Jerri Ledford & Rebecca Freshour*

Brilliant Microsoft® Word 2007 Pocket Book  *Deanna Reynolds*

# Contents

# Introduction

Welcome to the *Brilliant Microsoft® Access 2007 Pocket Book* – a handy visual quick reference that will give you a basic grounding in the common features and tasks that you will need to master to use Microsoft® Access 2007 in any day-to-day situation. Keep it on your desk, in your briefcase or bag – or even in your pocket! – and you will always have the answer to hand for any problem or task that you come across.

**Find out what you need to know – when you need it!**

You don't have to read this book in any particular order. It is designed so that you can jump in, get the information you need and jump out – just look up the task in the contents list, turn to the right page, read the introduction, follow the step-by-step instructions – and you're done!

## How this book works

Each section in this book includes foolproof step-by-step instructions for performing specific tasks, using screenshots to illustrate each step. Additional information is included to help increase your understanding and develop your skills – these are identified by the following icons:

 **Jargon buster** – New or unfamiliar terms are defined and explained in plain English to help you as you work through a section.

 **Timesaver tip** – These tips give you ideas that cut corners and confusion. They also give you additional information related to the topic that you are currently learning. Use them to expand your knowledge of a particular feature or concept.

 **Important** – This identifies areas where new users often run into trouble, and offers practical hints and solutions to these problems.

**Brilliant Pocket Books are a handy, accessible resource that you will find yourself turning to time and time again when you are faced with a problem or an unfamiliar task and need an answer at your fingertips – or in your pocket!**

# 1

# What's New in Access 2007

In this lesson, you will learn how to use the Ribbon, Quick Access Toolbar and Navigation pane in Microsoft Access 2007. You will also learn about new features to look for as you use this book.

# → Using the Ribbon

Microsoft Access 2007 is a database application that allows you to manage, track and share information by using data from different sources. This version of Access is much more intuitive than previous versions because it uses the Ribbon – a tabbed concept from Microsoft that makes finding and using commands logical and simple. Regardless of your experience level with Access, you will find this new interface makes good sense and is easy to follow.

The Ribbon takes the place of menus and toolbars previously used in Access. It is a bar across the top of your window. It uses a tab system to hold the commands you need and each tab is called a *command tab*. When you are working on a task or object, the specific command tab you are working with is referred to as a *contextual command tab*. This specific tab will contain the commands that apply to what you are currently doing in Access.

## Jargon buster

**Access objects** are the pieces that make up a database. These can include tables, forms, queries, and reports.

Figure 1.1 shows how the command tabs appear in the Ribbon of a newly opened Access database.

**Figure 1.1**
The Ribbon helps you to quickly find the command you need.

Within each command tab are specific command buttons, boxes and menus. These items are organised into logical groups. Notice in Figure 1.1, for example, that the Home tab is shown. Within the Home tab, there are seven groups: Views, Clipboard, Font, Rich Text, Records, Sort & Filter and Find.

Each of these groups holds a variety of commands related to the group name. To change the colour of your text, for example, you would use the Font group within the Home tab. Select the text you want changed, use the Font Color command and then select a new colour.

The commands in each group are the ones most commonly used. You may see a down arrow next to some commands; clicking on this will give you a short menu from which to choose additional commands. Some command groups, however, will also have a tiny, angled arrow located in the bottom right corner, as shown.

When you click on the arrow, a dialogue box will appear, offering you even more commands to choose from. Not every group has the dialogue box launcher. Take a quick look when you see one in a group so that you can get a good idea of which commands are launched and where.

The Ribbon responds to the actions you take. This means that you won't see every possible command within Access – you will see only the commands needed for the work you are performing. As you carry out different tasks, the command tabs will change depending on the action you are currently performing. This useful feature makes it easy to find what you're looking for.

## Taking Advantage of the Quick Access Toolbar

Immediately above the Ribbon is a small toolbar called the Quick Access Toolbar (Figure 1.2). This is customisable. It holds commands independently of the Ribbon so that you can quickly access commands that you use often.

**Figure 1.2**
The Quick Access Toolbar holds commands for fast access. It is easily customised.

The default commands on the Quick Access Toolbar are Save and Undo/Redo. You can use the Customise Quick Access Toolbar dropdown menu (Figure 1.3) to add commands that Microsoft deems the most commonly used. To add an item using the dropdown menu, follow these steps.

**1** Click on the **Customise Quick Access Toolbar** down arrow.

**2** Click on the item that you want to add to your toolbar.

**Figure 1.3**
A dropdown menu offers you a fast way to customise your Quick Access Toolbar.

A fast way to add other commands to the toolbar is to add them directly from the Ribbon. Follow these steps.

**1** Select the command you want to add. Right-click on it.

**2** Click on **Add to Quick Access Toolbar**.

## Timesaver tip

You can move the Quick Access Toolbar below the Ribbon if you prefer that location. Click on the **Customise Quick Access Toolbar** dropdown arrow, then click on **Show Below the Ribbon**.

There is one final way to add commands to your Quick Access Toolbar using the Access Options. The steps are a little more detailed, but not difficult. Follow these steps.

1 Click on the **Microsoft Office button** .

2 Click on **Access Options**. The dialogue box (shown in Figure 1.4) will appear.

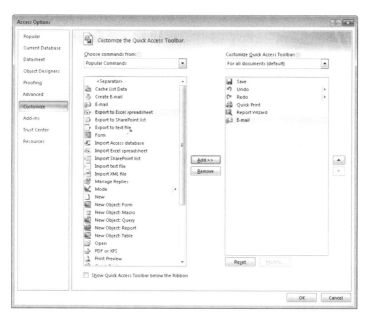

Figure 1.4

The Quick Access Toolbar can also be customised using the Access Options Customise command.

**3** Click on **Customise**.

**4** In **Choose commands from**, select the category where the commands you need are located.

**5** In the column directly below Choose commands from, select the command you want to add. Click on **Add**. The command will move to the column on the right. Continue adding commands as desired. If you make a mistake, select the item in the right-hand column and click on **Remove**.

**6** Click on **OK** when you are done.

## → Working with the Navigation Pane

Below the Ribbon is a new feature in Access 2007 – the Navigation pane. It's located on the left side of the window and visible at all times unless you decide to collapse it. Every object in a new or existing database will appear in this pane. By default, all the objects are placed into categories and then divided into Access groups, as shown in Figure 1.5.

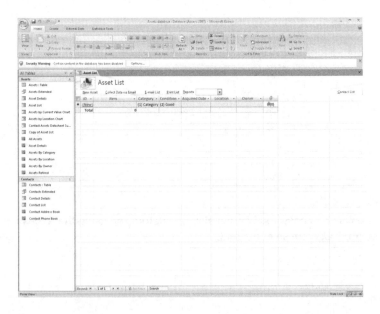

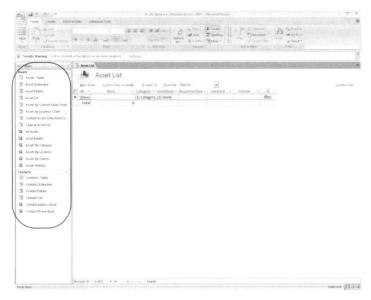

**Figure 1.5**
The Navigation pane displays all objects in a database by category
and group.

Tables and Related Views is the default category, the default
group for this category being All Tables. If an object is based on
more than one table, it will appear in the groups for each table.
You can group your objects differently by selecting another
category using the menu opened by the down arrow at the top of
the Navigation pane, as shown in Figure 1.6. You can also use up
and down arrows to collapse or expand a group.

**Timesaver tip**

The Navigation pane has replaced the switchboard previously used in
Access. This change means that you can now manage objects in a
database directly from the Navigation pane. Some switchboards
created in earlier versions of Access might work in Access 2007,
although limitations often occur.

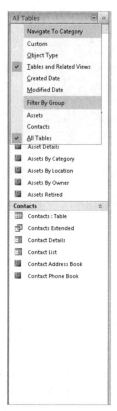

**Figure 1.6**
Categories are selected by using a drop-down menu in the Navigation pane.

The Navigation pane consists of five key areas, although you may not see that many at any given time. That's because some will only appear as needed. When you work within the Navigation pane, you are working with two items: database objects and the shortcuts to those objects.

The first three areas are the menu, groups and database objects, which we've already discussed. Next is the Shutter Bar Open/Close button located next to the menu. This button opens or collapses the Navigation pane. Finally, open space is considered a key area in Access 2007 because a right-click on the Navigation pane open space will open a menu that allows you to perform a variety of tasks for the objects in each group. As you use this book, you will see how the Navigation pane works in specific situations.

## → Other New Tools and Features to Watch For

Many of the improvements in Access 2007 make it easier for you to focus on the data you need rather than finding commands and menus. As you read through this book and work with Access on your own, watch for new features like the following:

- **AutoFilter** – lets you sort using plain language or by choosing unique values in a column

- **the TextFormat property** – lets you format text in many ways

- **a Totals row** – allows you to add count, sum, average, minimum, maximum, standard deviation or variance

- **a Field Templates pane** – designed to reduce the time you spend on design

- **a Field List pane** – can sense relationships between tables and help you with automatic creation of fields

- **a Split Form** – lets you combine Datasheet and Form Views

- **a Layout View** – allows you to make changes to design while viewing a live form or report

- **a QuickCreate option** – helps improve how your reports look

- **stacked and tabular layouts** – can be manipulated as one unit (including the label) and saved for reuse

- **automatic compression of attachments**

- **alternative colour options** – for your background

- **embedded macros** – help you to avoid writing code

■ **a Data Collection option** – automatically creates an HTML or Office InfoPath 2007 form and embeds it into your e-mail

■ **the ability to retain a history of all changes to a Memo field**

■ **the Move Data and Link to SharePoint Site Wizard** – let you subscribe to e-mail alerts from SharePoint sites.

# 2

# Access 2007 Fundamentals

In this lesson, you will learn how to open Access and identify the displays and function keys shown. You will also learn about the various views used in Access and how to exit a database and the program.

## → Opening Access

Access 2007 can be opened in several ways. You can open an individual database, for example, and the program will open that way. If you want to create a new database from scratch, however, you will use the Start button in Windows Vista. Follow these steps.

**1** Go to **Start**.

**2** Click on **All Programs**.

**3** Click on **Microsoft Office**.

**4** Click on **Microsoft Office Access 2007**.

Once Windows Vista has opened a program, it will place it in the Start menu to make it easier to find. However, if you open a lot of programs, Access 2007 will not stay in the Start menu unless you 'pin' it there. To pin Access 2007 into your Start menu, follow these steps after you have opened Access 2007.

**1** Go to **Start**.

**2** Right-click on **Microsoft Access 2007**.

**3** Click on **Pin to Start Menu**, as shown in Figure 2.1. This moves Access 2007 to the upper part of the Start menu where it will always be available to you when you click on Start.

You can also add Access 2007 to the Quick Launch menu next to your Start button. To do that, follow these steps.

**1** Go to **Start**.

**2** Locate **Microsoft Access 2007** and right-click on it.

**3** Click on **Add to Quick Launch**. This will place a shortcut icon on the Quick launch menu next to the Start button, as shown.

**Figure 2.1**
You can permanently place Access 2007 in your Start menu.

When you open Access 2007, you will see the Getting Started with Microsoft Access screen shown on the next page.

This screen provides you with several options for creating a database. They will be discussed in more detail in Chapters 5 and 6. For now, open the Northwind 2007 database. Depending on how much you have already played with Access 2007, this sample database could be located in several places on your screen. If you don't see it quickly, follow these steps to open it.

**1** Select **Local Templates** under **Template Categories**.

**2** Select **Northwind 2007** under **Local Templates** in the centre of your screen.

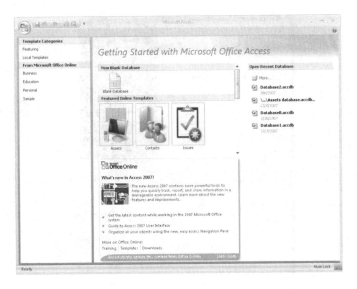

**3** Click on **Create** on the right side of your screen. The first time you do this, it might take a few minutes for the database template to appear.

Once the Northwind database has opened, you will see a Startup Screen. If a security warning appears just above that screen, follow these steps to enable all content in the database.

**1** Click on **Options**.

**2** Select **Enable this content**, shown here.

**3** Click on **OK**.

**4** When the **Login Dialogue box** appears, click on **Login**. It doesn't matter which employee you choose.

## Timesaver tip

Access 2007 offers you the option of creating a database from a template. The Getting Started with Microsoft Office Access screen offers multiple options for finding templates.

# → Function Keys

There are dozens of keyboard shortcut keys you can use with Access 2007. To learn all of them, take some time to read through the Help and Support information for Keyboard Shortcuts. Here, however, are several shortcuts that might come in handy as you begin working with Access 2007. Some shortcuts will only work in certain views or in certain areas of Access, so, if a shortcut mentioned here does not work for you, then you are not in the correct view or area of your database for it to function. Check Help and Support for more specific details in that case.

| Press | To perform this function |
|---|---|
| CTRL + N | Open a new database. |
| CTRL + O | Open an existing database. |
| ALT + F4 | Exit Access 2007. |
| CTRL + P | Print the current or selected object. |
| F12 | To open the Save As dialog box. |
| F11 | To open or close the Navigation pane. |
| F1 | Open Access 2007 Help and Support. |
| F4 | To switch to the property sheet. |
| F5 | Switch to Form view from the Design view. |
| F6 | Switch between upper and lower portions of a window or cycle through the areas in the Design view of a table. |

# → View Options

You can view information in a database in several different ways, depending on the information you're reviewing. There are four primary views in Access 2007: Form, Layout, Datasheet and Design. Each of these will be addressed throughout this book, but what follows is a brief overview.

■ **Form** – This view shows the actual form as readers will see it.

■ **Layout** – Using this view allows you to arrange data on the page. You can make design changes to forms as the data is displayed. This view is typically used to perform tasks that impact the appearance and usability of a form.

■ **Datasheet** – This view allows you to enter data, by typing, pasting or importing information. Data must be entered in contiguous rows and columns.

■ **Design** – This view is used to create a new table's structure and set field properties. It is a detailed view of the structure of your form, but the form is not actually running while you are in this view.

■ **Split form** – This is an additional view that lets you see the Form View and Datasheet View at the same time. Split forms are addressed in more detail in Chapter 18.

To change the view in a database, follow these steps.

**1** Go to the **Home tab**.

**2** Click on **View** in the **Views group**.

**3** Select the view you want to see.

# → Saving in Access

You can save database files in Access very easily. To save a database created in Access 2007, follow these steps.

**1** Click on the **Microsoft Office button**.

**2** Point to **Save As** and click on **Access 2007 Database**, as shown here.

**3** A warning will tell you that all open objects must be closed prior to converting to a different version. Click on **Yes**.

**4** In the **Save As** window, type in the name you want to use for the database in **File Name**.

**5** The **Save As** type should be Microsoft Office Access 2007 Database (*.accdb).

**6** Click on **Save**.

For more information on file formats in Access 2007, see Chapter 4.

# → Exiting Access

You can exit Access 2007 using the Microsoft Office button.
Before you exit any database, be certain that you have saved it.
Then, follow these steps.

**1** Click on the **Microsoft Office button**.

**2** Click on **Exit Access**.

## Timesaver tip

Exit Access in just one step by clicking on the **quick close button**
located at the top right of the Access window (the **X**).

# 3

# Understanding Access 2007

In this lesson, you will discover the key elements of an Access 2007 database. These elements will be used as references and examples throughout this book and with most databases you develop, so it's important to have a basic understanding of them.

# → Databases and Objects

A *database* is really just a collection of pieces of information stored in a logical, structured format on a computer. These pieces of information are stored as records that can be easily consulted and retrieved. Outlook 2007, for example, uses a database to store contacts for you.

A *database object* identifies where and how the information is stored. An Access 2007 database object could be a column, table, view, report, macro, module or form. You can save objects in multiple ways – you might have a form that is also accessible in a table, for instance.

# → Tables

Access 2007 organises information into *tables*, which are really just lists of rows and columns. In a very simple database, just one table might be used. In complex databases, dozens of tables can be created to store all the information that you have.

Tables are similar in appearance to spreadsheets, but the data is organised differently. Instead of storing all your information on a single spreadsheet, tables allow you to store pieces of information individually.

Each row in a table is called a *record*. Each record can have multiple columns, which are called *fields*. For example, a 'Customer' table might have separate customer records (rows) that have various fields (columns) containing address, phone number, job title and other information, as shown in Figure 3.1.

| ID | Company | Last Name | First Name | Job Title | Business Ph | Fax Number | Address | City | State/Provir | ZIP/Postal C | Country/Reg | Web |
|---|---|---|---|---|---|---|---|---|---|---|---|---|
| 1 | Company A | Bedecs | Anna | Owner | (123)555-0100 | (123)555-0101 | 123 1st Street | Seattle | WA | 99999 | USA | |
| 2 | Company B | Gratacos Solso | Antonio | Owner | (123)555-0100 | (123)555-0101 | 123 2nd Street | Boston | MA | 99999 | USA | |
| 3 | Company C | Axen | Thomas | Purchasing Representati | (123)555-0100 | (123)555-0101 | 123 3rd Street | Los Angelas | CA | 99999 | USA | |
| 4 | Company D | Lee | Christina | Purchasing Manager | (123)555-0100 | (123)555-0101 | 123 4th Street | New York | NY | 99999 | USA | |
| 5 | Company E | O'Donnell | Martin | Owner | (123)555-0100 | (123)555-0101 | 123 5th Street | Minneapolis | MN | 99999 | USA | |
| 6 | Company F | Pérez-Olaeta | Francisco | Purchasing Manager | (123)555-0100 | (123)555-0101 | 123 6th Street | Milwaukee | WI | 99999 | USA | |
| 7 | Company G | Xie | Ming-Yang | Owner | (123)555-0100 | (123)555-0101 | 123 7th Street | Boise | ID | 99999 | USA | |
| 8 | Company H | Andersen | Elizabeth | Purchasing Representati | (123)555-0100 | (123)555-0101 | 123 8th Street | Portland | OR | 99999 | USA | |
| 9 | Company I | Mortensen | Sven | Purchasing Manager | (123)555-0100 | (123)555-0101 | 123 9th Street | Salt Lake City | UT | 99999 | USA | |
| 10 | Company J | Wacker | Roland | Purchasing Manager | (123)555-0100 | (123)555-0101 | 123 10th Street | Chicago | IL | 99999 | USA | |
| 11 | Company K | Krschne | Peter | Purchasing Manager | (123)555-0100 | (123)555-0101 | 123 11th Street | Miami | FL | 99999 | USA | |
| 12 | Company L | Edwards | John | Purchasing Manager | (123)555-0100 | (123)555-0101 | 123 12th Street | Las Vegas | NV | 99999 | USA | |
| 13 | Company M | Ludick | Andre | Purchasing Representati | (123)555-0100 | (123)555-0101 | 456 13th Street | Memphis | TN | 99999 | USA | |
| 14 | Company N | Grilo | Carlos | Purchasing Representati | (123)555-0100 | (123)555-0101 | 456 14th Street | Denver | CO | 99999 | USA | |
| 15 | Company O | Kupkova | Helena | Purchasing Manager | (123)555-0100 | (123)555-0101 | 456 15th Street | Honolulu | HI | 99999 | USA | |
| 16 | Company P | Goldschmidt | Daniel | Purchasing Representati | (123)555-0100 | (123)555-0101 | 456 16th Street | San Francisco | CA | 99999 | USA | |
| 17 | Company Q | Bagel | Jean Philippe | Owner | (123)555-0100 | (123)555-0101 | 456 17th Street | Seattle | WA | 99999 | USA | |
| 18 | Company R | Autier Miconi | Catherine | Purchasing Representati | (123)555-0100 | (123)555-0101 | 456 18th Street | Boston | MA | 99999 | USA | |
| 19 | Company S | Eggerer | Alexander | Accounting Assistant | (123)555-0100 | (123)555-0101 | 789 19th Street | Los Angelas | CA | 99999 | USA | |
| 20 | Company T | Li | George | Purchasing Manager | (123)555-0100 | (123)555-0101 | 789 20th Street | New York | NY | 99999 | USA | |
| 21 | Company U | Tham | Bernard | Accounting Manager | (123)555-0100 | (123)555-0101 | 789 21th Street | Minneapolis | MN | 99999 | USA | |
| 22 | Company V | Ramos | Luciana | Purchasing Assistant | (123)555-0100 | (123)555-0101 | 789 22th Street | Milwaukee | WI | 99999 | USA | |
| 23 | Company W | Entin | Michael | Purchasing Manager | (123)555-0100 | (123)555-0101 | 789 23th Street | Portland | OR | 99999 | USA | |
| 24 | Company X | Hasselberg | Jonas | Owner | (123)555-0100 | (123)555-0101 | 789 24th Street | Salt Lake City | UT | 99999 | USA | |
| 25 | Company Y | Rodman | John | Purchasing Manager | (123)555-0100 | (123)555-0101 | 789 25th Street | Chicago | IL | 99999 | USA | |
| 26 | Company Z | Liu | Run | Accounting Assistant | (123)555-0100 | (123)555-0101 | 789 26th Street | Miami | FL | 99999 | USA | |
| 27 | Company AA | Toh | Karen | Purchasing Manager | (123)555-0100 | (123)555-0101 | 789 27th Street | Las Vegas | NV | 99999 | USA | |
| 28 | Company BB | Raghav | Amritansh | Purchasing Manager | (123)555-0100 | (123)555-0101 | 789 28th Street | Memphis | TN | 99999 | USA | |
| 29 | Company CC | Lee | Soo Jung | Purchasing Manager | (123)555-0100 | (123)555-0101 | 789 29th Street | Denver | CO | 99999 | USA | |
| | [New] | | | | | | | | | | | |

**Figure 3.1**
Rows and columns in an Access table are referred to as records and fields.

# → Forms

Forms are used to enter data and perform various commands. You don't need to use forms in your database, but it does make it easier to view, enter and edit data in Access tables.

For example, maybe you have a form called "Employees", in which all your employees data is kept. A command button can be programmed and added to the form so that with a single click you can open a new form called "Vacation accrual" to track the number of vacation days of individual employees.

Forms are also very useful when you know that others will be accessing your database as you can create forms that show only certain fields and allow only specific actions to be completed by others. This helps you to control the accuracy and integrity of your data.

# → Queries

You will use the query feature in Access often. That's because it can perform a variety of functions that can help you to retrieve information from your database – it's a method for asking questions and receiving back the answers.

Often, the data you need will be spread across many different tables. Queries take the information from all those tables and drop it into a single datasheet so that you can see all the information. You can filter the data that a query returns so you only see specific information. For example, perhaps you need to know how many of a specific product are on order. A query can show you that quickly and easily.

There are two types of queries: a *select query* retrieves the data you request, while an *action query* retrieves the data you request plus it performs a task that you designate.

### Timesaver tip

With the Query Wizard in Access 2007, you can quickly create four different types of queries.

# → Reports

Reports are used to summarise and present the data from your tables. Typically, a report answers a specific question that you ask. Maybe you want to know the cities where your customers are located. A report can gather that information and then present it in an easy-to-read format, as shown.

## Customer Cities

| City | Last Name | Job Title | Company |
|------|-----------|-----------|---------|
| Boise | Xie | Owner | Company G |
| Boston | Autier Miconi | Purchasing Representative | Company R |
| Boston | Gratacos Solsona | Owner | Company B |
| Chicago | Rodman | Purchasing Manager | Company Y |
| Chicago | Wacker | Purchasing Manager | Company J |
| Denver | Grilo | Purchasing Representative | Company N |
| Denver | Lee | Purchasing Manager | Company CC |
| Honolulu | Kupkova | Purchasing Manager | Company O |
| Las Vegas | Edwards | Purchasing Manager | Company L |
| Las Vegas | Toh | Purchasing Manager | Company AA |
| Los Angeles | Axen | Purchasing Representative | Company C |
| Los Angeles | Eggerer | Accounting Assistant | Company S |
| Memphis | Ludick | Purchasing Representative | Company M |
| Memphis | Raghav | Purchasing Manager | Company BB |

Reports can be run whenever you want and can be printed, viewed on the screen, exported to other programs or sent as e-mails.

## → Macros

A *macro* is a very cool little piece of programming that contains actions to perform tasks. For instance, a macro could be created to run a query that you often use. Instead of continually setting up the same query over and over again, a macro will instantly set up and run the query for you at the click of a button. Almost all database operations can be automated in this way by means of macros. These are provided in the form of a list of actions in Access.

# → Modules

*Modules* are similar to macros but require that you write the actual program using Visual Basic for Applications (VBA), a programming language. Most people don't use modules because of the complexity involved.

**Important**

In other Office 2007 programs, the term "macro" is used to refer to VBA code. Don't let that confuse you as you use Access 2007, however. In this program, the term "macro" applies *only* to the specific list of actions provided in the Macro Builder.

# → The Sandbox Operating Mode

Access 2007 typically works in an operating environment called *sandbox mode*. This mode is set by default and helps to protect your computer by blocking all expressions considered unsafe. For example, an unsafe expression such as 'Kill' is a function within a database that could be used by someone to maliciously gain access to your computer's hard drives or other files.

The sandbox mode will always block these types of expressions unless you specifically disable the mode. When you trust the source of the database, you can change a registry key to allow a particular unsafe expression to still run.

**Important**

A database must have a valid trust signature or be located in a trusted location in order to disable sandbox mode.

# → Changing the Registry Key

**3**

## Important

Before beginning this process, enable the content in the database in which you are changing the registry key.

**1** Close any Access database for which you want to disable the sandbox mode.

In Windows Vista,

**2** Click on the **Start button** and point to **All Programs**.

**3** Click on **Accessories**.

**4** Click on **Run**. In the **Run dialogue box**, type 'regedit'.

**5** Click on **OK**.

**6** In the **Registry Editor window** that opens, expand the HKEY_LOCAL_MACHINE folder in the left pane and navigate to the following registry key: \Software\Microsoft\Office\12.0\Access Connectivity Engine\Engines

**7** In the right pane, double-click on **SandboxMode** under **Name**.

**8** When the **Edit DWORD Value dialog box** appears, change the value from **3** to **2** in the **Value Data field**.

**9** Click on **OK**.

**10** Close the **Registry Editor**.

## Timesaver tip

Registry values range from 0 (most permissive) to 3 (least permissive). Use 0 to disable the sandbox mode at all times, use 1 to keep the sandbox mode for Access 2007 but no other programs, 2 to set the sandbox mode for non-Access programs but *not* Access and 3 to set the sandbox mode for use at all times and with all programs.

# 4

# The New File Format

In this lesson, you will learn about the new file format in Access 2007 and how to convert files from earlier versions of Access into Access 2007 files.

# → Understanding the New File Format

There is a new file format to be aware of when you save files in Access 2007. The new default file format is *.accdb*. Previous versions of Access used the file extension .mdb.

The new file format supports features such as multivalued fields, attachment data types, improved encryption methods and memo field history tracking. It also provides stronger integration with Windows SharePoint Services and Microsoft Office Outlook 2007.

**Jargon buster**

**Encryption** is a process for turning plain text into non-readable information so that sensitive data remains secure.

Multivalued fields let you select and store more than one choice for a field without an advanced database design. These integrate well with Microsoft Windows SharePoint Services 3.0. The attachment data types feature automatically compressed attachments stored in your database to maximise space. Memo field history tracking is a feature that retains a history of all changes to a Memo field in a database so you can see what happened and when.

While Access 2007 does offer some support for the file format offered in earlier versions of Access, converting files to the new format will provide all the newest features and functions available. For example, you can't make design changes to a file in Access 95 or Access 97 format when you open it in Access 2007.

## Timesaver tip

You can open Access files with the .mdb extension in Access 2007 but may not always be able to take advantage of the newer features offered by Access 2007. Files saved in the new .accdb format cannot be opened by earlier versions of Access.

**4**

If you work with other people who have not yet upgraded to Access 2007, you can still save the database as a .mdb file.

## → Converting a Database into an Access 2007 File

To convert a database created in an earlier version of Access into an Access 2007 file, open Access and then follow these steps.

**1** Click on the **Microsoft Office button**.

**2** Click on **Open**.

**3** In the **Open dialogue box**, select and open the database that you want to convert.

When the database is open,

**4** Click on the **Microsoft Office button** and then point to **Save As**.

**5** Under **Save the database in another format**, click on **Access 2007 Database**.

**6** In the **Save As dialogue box**, in the **File Name** box, enter a file name or use the file name supplied.

**7** Click on **Save**.

# 5

# Database Fundamentals

In this lesson, you will learn the concepts you need to know to design a database. Specific instructions for the design aspects mentioned here are covered in related sections of this book – this chapter provides an overview only.

# → Understanding Databases

As mentioned earlier in this book, a *database* is really just a collection of pieces of information stored in a logical, structured format on a computer. The pieces of information are stored as records that can be easily consulted and retrieved.

Effective design is critical when creating a database – it makes it easier for you to retrieve accurate, consistent and complete information.

# → Designing a Database

When you design a database, create one that uses subject-based tables to reduce redundant data and gives Access the information it needs to connect information from multiple tables as needed.

Think about the results you expect from the database. Will you need to run specific reports for executives? Will you need to produce mass mailings from it? Designing with the end result in mind will help you determine what is the right information to include in your database.

**Timesaver tip**

Before you create a database, clearly outline its purpose. This will help you find and organise the information you need to best meet your purpose – and will keep you from going off-track with your design.

### Setting up Primary Categories

Once you have all the information you need for your database, take a few minutes to divide it into major categories, such as Customers or Inventory. As you create the database, these categories should be separate tables.

## Adding Subcategories

Within each category, further subdivide the information so that you can decide which details should go into which table. For example, if you have a Customers table, will you also have addresses, phone numbers, billing details? Each of these subcategories should be a field within your table.

## Choosing Primary Keys

For each table, create a primary key – this is the first column that is used to uniquely identify each row, such as 'Status ID', as shown here.

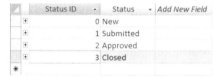

| | Status ID | ▾ | Status | ▾ | Add New Field |
|---|---|---|---|---|---|
| ⊞ | | 0 | New | | |
| ⊞ | | 1 | Submitted | | |
| ⊞ | | 2 | Approved | | |
| ⊞ | | 3 | Closed | | |
| * | | | | | |

## Establishing Table Relationships

Once you have set up all your tables, you need to determine how each table relates to data in other tables. For example, does a customer table need to use information from a products table? If so, you will need to add fields to your tables (or set up new tables) to create the proper relationships.

## Analysing the Design

It's a good idea to add sample data into your design and test the database to see whether or not you can retrieve the information you expect. This step will save you a lot of time as, if you add in all your data before you analyse the design, you might find errors that require database design adjustments – and the re-entering of data.

Adjust the design as needed until you are confident that the design will meet your original purpose for the database.

# 6

# Creating a Database

In this lesson, you will learn how to create a database, whether you are starting from scratch or working with a template. You'll also learn how to open existing databases and copy and close databases.

## → Creating a New, Blank Database

When you want to create a database by building your own tables, forms and other objects, you must create a new blank database. This process can involve importing, pasting or entering data into an initial table in your new database, then repeating the process using new tables until you have all the tables you need.

**Timesaver tip**

When you import data from external sources, you usually don't have to create a table for it. This is because Access will do that automatically as it imports the information.

To create a new, blank database, follow these steps.

**1** Open Access 2007. On the **Getting Started with Microsoft Office Access** page, click on **Blank Database** under **New Blank Database**, as shown in Figure 6.1.

**Timesaver tip**

You can also get to the **Getting Started** screen from within an open Access database by clicking on the **Microsoft Office button** and then on **New**.

**2** Under **Blank Database** in the right pane, type in the name you wish to give the new database under **File Name**. Access will automatically give the file the file format extension of .accdb unless you supply a different file name extension.

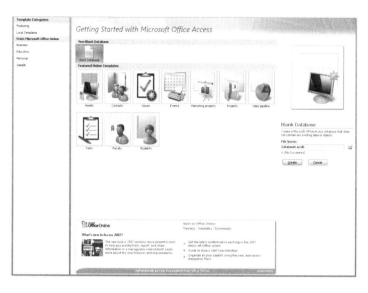

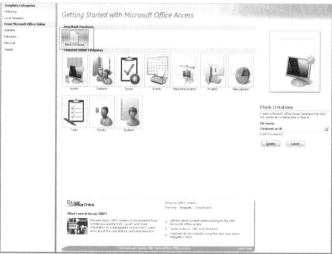

**Figure 6.1**
New, blank databases are located on the Getting Started with
Microsoft Office Access page.

**3** Notice that immediately underneath the file name, the
**location** of the file is listed. If you wish to change the location,
click on the yellow folder to the right of the file name and
browse to the location you prefer, as shown. Click on **OK**.

**Blank Database**

Create a Microsoft Office Access database that does not contain any existing data or objects.

File **N**ame:

Brilliant Sample

U:\My Documents\

Create    Cancel

---

**4** Under **Blank Database**, click on **Create**. A blank database will appear. An empty table called **Table1** will be shown in the **Datasheet View**. The **Add New Field** column will be highlighted and your cursor is automatically placed in this column. You can begin entering your information by typing it in or pasting it from another source.

### Timesaver tip

In Access, the table structure is created as you enter data. Each time you add a new column to the table, a new field is defined. Access instantly sets each field's data type based on the data you enter. For more details on creating tables, see Chapters 10 to 15.

## → Creating a Database from a Template

Many people prefer to use existing templates to create a database rather than generate new ones. With this method, you simply open pre-made databases provided by Access and then change the tables by adding or removing fields as needed. It's a fast and simple way to create a database because most of the work has already been done for you – you simply provide the information for it.

To create a new database using a template, follow these steps.

**1** Open Access 2007. On the **Getting Started with Microsoft Office Access** page, click on **Local Templates** under **Template Categories**, as shown in Figure 6.2.

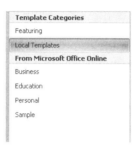

**Figure 6.2**
Access 2007 provides pre-built templates to make it easy to create new databases.

**2** Click on a template from the list provided. As you do, notice that, in the right pane, details about the template will appear, along with a default file name and location. Click through the templates until you find one that you like (see below).

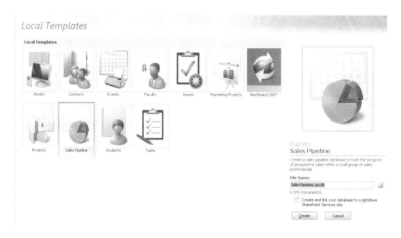

**3** Once you locate a template that you wish to use, enter the new **file name** and **location** (use the yellow folder icon to browse for a new location).

**4** Click on **Create**. It might take a few seconds for Access to prepare the template for use. Then, a database with pre-built tables will appear. You can begin to enter your information by typing it into the tables provided or pasting it in from other sources. You can always create new tables in a template as well.

**Timesaver tip**

If the Navigation pane is closed when your template opens, simply click on the shutter bar open/close button at the top of the pane to open it.

## → Opening an Existing Database

If you already have an existing database and need to open it, follow these steps.

**1** Click on the **Microsoft Office button** from within an existing database.

**2** Click on **Open**.

**3** Locate and select the database you want to open. Click on **Open**.

You can also open an existing database by following these steps.

**1** Open Access 2007.

**2** On the **Getting Started with Microsoft Office Access** page, click on the database that you want to open under **Open Recent Database**.

**3** If you do not see the database you need, click on **More** to browse for the database on your computer.

## Important

If you work in a multi-user environment and are concerned about version control with your database, click on the **arrow** next to the Open button `Open ▼` in the **Open dialogue box**. Click **Open Exclusive**. Anyone else who attempts to open the same database while you are using it will receive the message 'file already in use' and be unable to open the database.

# → Copying a Database 6

If you need to make a copy of your database, follow these steps.

**1** Open the database you want to make a copy of.

**2** Click on the **Microsoft Office button**. Point to **Save As**.

**3** Click on **Access 2007 Database**.

**4** Click on **Yes**.

**5** In the **Save As dialogue box**, type in the new name for the copy of your database under **File Name**. Be sure to check that you are saving it to the correct location.

**6** Click on **Save**.

## Jargon buster

The **Security Warning** notice (below) is shown when certain content in a database has been automatically disabled by Access. Click on **Options** to see the specific security alert, then make your choice as to whether or not to enable the content or keep it disabled.

> ⚠ **Security Warning**   Certain content in the database has been disabled   `Options...`

# → Closing a Database

To close a database but still keep Access open, follow these steps.

**1** In the open database, click on the **Microsoft Office button**.

**2** Click on **Close Database**. Access will remain open and you will be taken to the **Getting Started with Microsoft Office Access** page.

# 7

# Publishing a Database to a SharePoint Site

In this lesson, you will learn how to publish a database to a SharePoint site.

# → What are SharePoint Services?

Microsoft offers SharePoint Server 2007, which is an integrated suite of capabilities offered via a single platform. Businesses are most likely to use the product, individuals typically do not need it. If your business uses SharePoint Services, you probably have access to a SharePoint website. This site is a central location where people within your organisation can post and retrieve documents. For example, you may need to post an Access database so that others in your organisation can open it to analyse and review the information it contains.

## Important

Only database files saved in the Office Access 2007 file format can be published to a SharePoint site.

When people open a database you have posted to the site, the objects you created are available to readers on a read-only basis. However, they can simply save the database as a local copy and then make changes if they wish. No changes are recorded on the SharePoint site, however, unless they republish the database to it.

It is possible to create an Access database on a SharePoint site, too. If you need to do this, check with your network administrator for instructions.

To publish a database to a SharePoint site, follow these steps.

**1** Click on the **Microsoft Office button** and point to **Publish**, as shown.

**2** Click on **Document Management Server**.

**3** Type the URL of the SharePoint site where you want the database to be published.

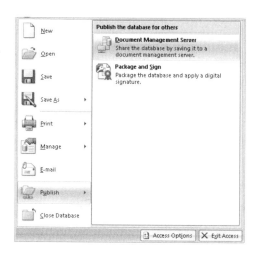

**4** Select the library where you want to publish the database.

**5** Click on **Open**.

**6** In the **Name** box, type in the file name for your database.

**7** Click on **Publish**.

# 8

# Finding Information in Your Database

In this lesson, you will learn how to find and replace information in your database easily and quickly.

## → Finding Words or Phrases

Access 2007 offers a Find and Replace feature that is similar to Find and Replace in other Office 2007 programs and helps you to quickly locate text within your database. For instance, maybe you need to find all occurrences of the word 'customer' in your database so that you can change the word to 'client' instead.

### Important

This feature searches only one table at a time, not the entire database. If you need to search multiple tables, use a query instead.

As it is used within a database, this feature differs slightly from other Office 2007 programs. It offers additional functions to make it more useful when searching relational databases.

### Timesaver tip

The Find and Replace feature is used instead of the query feature when you need to find and potentially replace small amounts of data.

To find data within a table, follow these steps.

**1** Select the table you want to search.

**2** Within that table, select the **field** (column) that you want to search.

**3** Go to the **Home tab** and click on **Find** in the **Find group**, as shown.

**4** The **Find dialogue box** will appear, as shown in Figure 8.1. Click on the **Find tab**. In **Find What**, type the word or phrase that you want to find.

Figure 8.1
The Find and Replace dialogue box in Access 2007.

**5** In the **Look In box**, select the field that you want to search. You can also choose to select the entire table here.

**6** In the **Match box**, select **Any Part of Field** for a broad search.

**7** In the **Search box**, select **All**.

**8** Be sure **Search Fields as Formatted** is selected.

**9** Click on **Find Next**.

**Important**

The Find and Replace dialogue box has an option called Search Fields As Formatted. Sometimes, Access checks this box automatically. If it does, it's not usually necessary to remove the check – if you do, your search operation may not return any results at all.

If you don't have permission to view or search a table – or if you don't want others to see data within a specific table – you can run Find and Replace on forms from both Form view and Layout view. Both methods search the original table attached to the form.

To find and replace data within a form, follow these steps.

**1** Open the form that you want to search. Be sure that it is in either the **Form** or **Layout View**.

**2** Select the control that contains the information to be searched.

**3** Go to the **Home tab** and click on **Find** in the **Find group**.

> **!**
>
> **Important**
>
> It is possible to launch the Find and Replace function, yet not be able to use the Replace feature. This happens when you are in a table or field that does not allow changes.

## → Replacing Words or Phrases

To replace data within a table or form, follow these steps after you have opened the Find and Replace dialogue box.

**1** Select the **Replace tab** in the **Find and Replace dialogue box**.

**2** Be sure that the word or phrase you want to find is in the **Find What box**.

**3** Enter the word or phrase you want to replace the original word or phrase with, as shown.

**4** Click on **Replace**.

**5** Click on **Find Next** and replace text as needed throughout the table or form.

## Jargon buster

**Find v. Filter  Finding** is the process of locating one or more records in database queries, forms and tables. **Filtering** is the process of displaying records based on certain conditions. Typically, data is first found and then filtered.

**8**

# 9

# Collecting Information Using Outlook 2007

In this lesson, you will learn about electronic data collection in Access 2007 and how to use it in conjunction with Outlook 2007.

# → When to Use Electronic Data Collection

Obtaining accurate and up-to-date information for your database has been improved in Access 2007. A new feature – Collect data through e-mail messages – can literally save you hours of time. Instead of manually entering data into your database, you can generate and send an e-mail data entry form to other people. When they fill out the form and e-mail it back to you, the replies are processed automatically to your Access database and entered into the table(s) you specify.

This feature can be used for a variety of situations, but is particularly useful for things such as surveys, status reports and event management activities. For example, you can send out a survey and have the answers sent directly to your database. Alternatively, you could have team members send you e-mail messages at regular intervals to keep a database up to date concerning sales information or similar items. If you are managing an event, you can gather travel and hotel preferences or contact information automatically, too.

**!**

### Important

To use this feature, you must have Outlook 2007 installed and configured on the same computer that you use to send the e-mail messages. Recipients of your e-mail must have an e-mail client that supports the HTML format – they don't need Outlook 2007.

# → Things to Know Before You Collect Electronic Data

Before you start this process, be sure that you have a destination database for the replies. The database can be in either .mdb or

.accdb file format. If you aren't using an existing database, you will need to create a new one.

The next step is to identify (or create) the tables you want the replies to go into. Most of the time, you can store the collected data as a new record or use it to update an existing record. There are four situations, however, when the data can only be stored as a new record. These are when:

■ data is being used to populate two or more tables

■ the underlying table of a form or other object does not have a primary key field

■ the underlying table is empty (no records have been set up)

■ the e-mail addresses of your recipients are not stored as an address field in the destination table – or in a table that has a relationship with the destination table.

A few more housekeeping items must be checked before you start the E-mail Collection Wizard. Outlook must be running to receive and process replies and your database should not be open in Exclusive mode or password protected. In addition, be certain that the location and name of the database is exactly what you want – if you change it after you send the e-mail, replies will not be processed by Access.

**Important**

Tables *cannot* be read-only and you must have the necessary permissions to add or update table content. Tables and queries – and all related properties – cannot be changed after sending the e-mail message. If any of these conditions are not met, Access cannot electronically update your database.

## → Collecting Data Via the E-mail Collection Wizard

Once you know where you want replies to go, it's time to start the E-mail Collection Wizard so that you can collect your data.

### Timesaver tip

You cannot use this feature to populate the fields Attachment, AutoNumber, Multi-valued, Object Linking and Embedding (OLE). To save time, check to be sure that the fields you choose are not one of these.

To start the Wizard, follow these steps.

**1** Open the destination database.

**2** If you are populating a *single* table with the replies, select the destination table in the **Navigation pane**. If you are populating *two or more tables* with the replies, select the **query** that is bound to those tables (see Chapters 29 to 34 for more details about queries).

**3** Go to the **External Data tab** and click on **Create E-mail** in the **Collect Data group**, as shown.

### Timesaver tip

You can also right-click a table or query and then click on **Collect data through e-mail messages** to create your e-mail.

When the Wizard starts, it will walk you through the steps and you just click on **Next** as you complete each step. You can return to a previous step by clicking on **Back**. If you are adding and updating data, there will be six steps to complete; otherwise there are five steps. In the example shown in Figure 9.1, only records are being added so the 'Update existing information' step is not covered.

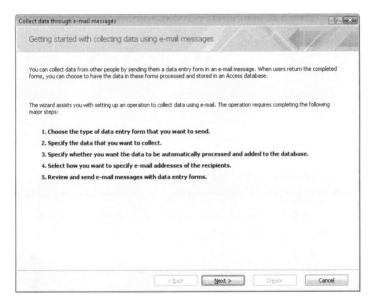

**Figure 9.1**
The opening page of the E-mail Collection Wizard.

With the Wizard open on its first page (see Figure 9.1), follow these steps to complete the process.

**1** Click on **Next**.

**2** Select the type of form that you want to e-mail. This is usually an HTML form. Microsoft Office InfoPath forms are available if both you and your recipients have that program. If InfoPath is greyed out as shown, you do not have that program installed. Click on **Next**.

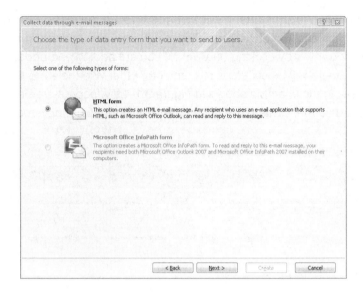

**3** Select the fields that you want to include in your form by highlighting a field and using the add or remove arrows in the centre of the Wizard to include it in the e-mail, as shown in Figure 9.2. Click on **Next**.

### Timesaver tip

Use the up and down arrows to the right of the Fields to include in e-mail message box to move your selected fields to different locations in the form.

**4** Select **Automatically Process Replies and Add Data to [your table or query will be named here]**.

**5** Click on **Set properties** to control the automatic processing of replies. This launches the **Import Settings dialogue box**.

**6** Select the settings you prefer. Click on **Next**.

**7** Select whether you are using e-mail addresses from Outlook 2007 or from a field within your database. Click on **Next**.

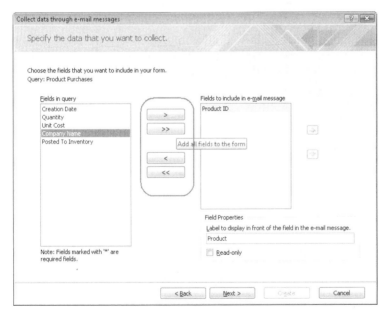

**Figure 9.2**
Fields are added to the e-mail by using add and remove arrows.

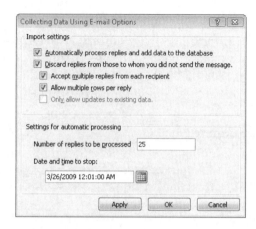

**8** Enter a subject line for your e-mail and include any additional information for the recipients, as shown in Figure 9.3. Click on **Next**.

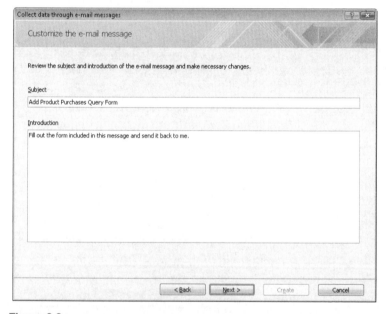

Figure 9.3
You have an opportunity to personalise your e-mail message as you walk through the Wizard.

**9** Click on **Create**. The e-mail message will appear on your screen for you to review, as shown here.

**10** Add your recipients to the e-mail. Click on **Send**.

### Important

Replies are stored in the Access Data Collection Replies folder of your Microsoft Office Outlook mailbox.

## → Managing Your Data Collection Replies

You can manage the data collection messages and replies very easily via the Manage Data Collection Messages dialogue box. To open this dialogue box, follow these steps.

**1** Open the database for the messages you want to manage.

**2** Go to the **External Data tab** and click on **Manage Replies** in the **Collect Data group**.

**3** When the **Manage Data Collection Messages dialogue box** launches, you will be able to review the message details, view or change message options, resend the message and/or delete the message. Choose the task you want to perform or simply review the information. When you have finished, click on **Close**.

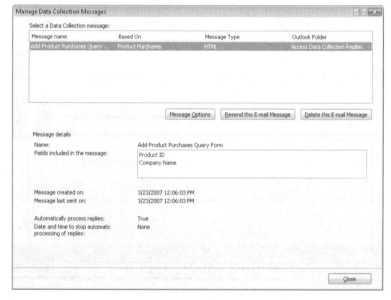

Figure 9.4

The Manage Data Collection Messages dialogue box can help you to manage the data collection messages that you send.

# 10

# Table Relationships and Design

In this lesson, you will learn about table relationships, which are essential to creating a useful, accurate database. This lesson explains how to design a table, as well as how to create, change and delete table relationships.

# → Understanding Table Relationships

There are many, many ways to work with table relationships, although there are just three primary types of table relationships to understand in Access 2007.

■ **One-to-many** — One side of this relationship has many fields. For example, a customer tracking database might have a Customer table and a Products table. As one customer can purchase many different products, the relationship between the two tables is called a one-to-many relationship (one employee, many product relationships). Creating a one-to-many relationship can be done by taking the primary key on the 'one' side of the relationship and adding it as an additional field on the 'many' side of the relationship.

■ **Many-to-many** — Both sides of this relationship have many relationships. For example, a single customer might order many products or a single product can appear on many customers' orders, establishing many customer relationships and many product relationships. In this type of table relationship, a junction table is created to break down the many-to-many relationships into as many one-to-many relationships as are needed.

■ **One-to-one** — Each side of this relationship has just one matching record connecting it to the other. This type of relationship is unusual, so you won't see it too often.

In the Northwind Traders database, you can view some sample table relationships by following the steps (you can use these steps in any Access 2007 database).

**1** Select a table.

**2** Go to the **Database Tools tab**. Click on **Relationships** in the **Show/Hide group, as shown**.

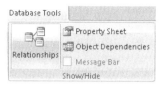

You should see a relationship table similar to the one shown in Figure 10.1. Take a few minutes to review it and understand how the tables all relate to one another. This step will help you as you design tables for your own databases.

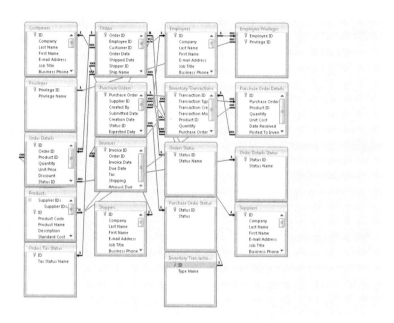

**Figure 10.1**
It's easy to view table relationships in Access 2007.

10

## → Designing a Table

When you design a table, it's important to decide beforehand what kind of information should be in a particular table – and to keep all tables as factually based as possible. This will help you to determine what the *major subjects* in your table are, as well as the *supporting subjects*.

### Important

In every table, include a column or set of columns that uniquely identifies the individual rows stored in the table. This is typically a unique identification number, such as an employee ID number or a product code. This is called the *primary key* of the table. It should be a value that does not change so that other tables can always sync to it.

For example, if you decide that a *major subject* in your table should be 'Customers', then what kind of information do you want to include about those customers? *Supporting subjects* could be name, address, city, country or region, post code, telephone and e-mail address.

As you consider your major and supporting subjects, avoid the temptation to place all the information in a single table. If you want to know which products a customer typically orders, for instance, do not make 'Products' a supporting subject under 'Customers'. Instead, create a second table called 'Products', then create a relationship between the Customer and Products tables. Using this relationship approach will keep you from entering duplicate information and save you time.

### Timesaver tip

Once you have defined the initial set of columns (supporting subjects) for your table, take some time to refine them. Store customer names, for instance, in two separate columns for first and last names. This approach will make it easier to sort, search and index your database later on.

It's helpful to write down the major and supporting subjects in a list format before you get started – it will help you to keep track of all the information and ensure that you don't forget anything as you create tables and table relationships.

# → Creating a Table Relationship

Once you have set up your information as tables, you can create relationships between them. Follow these steps to create a table relationship:

**1** Open the database you want to create the relationships in.

**2** Click on the **Microsoft Office button**.

**3** Click on **Open**.

**4** Go to the **Database Tools tab** and click on **Relationships** in the **Show/Hide group**.

**5** The **Show Table dialogue box** will appear if you have not yet defined any table relationships in the database. If you have defined some, go to the **Design tab** and click on **Show Table** in the **Relationships group**, as shown.

**6** In the **Show Table dialogue box**, you can select to see only tables, queries or both. For the purposes of these instructions, click on the **Both tab**.

**7** Select one or more tables and/or queries. Click on **Add**, as shown.

10

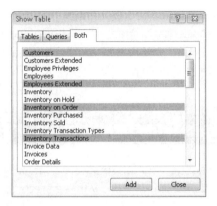

## Timesaver tip

Hold down the **Control button** on your keyboard as you make your selections in the **Show Table dialogue box**. This allows you to select multiple items at once.

**8** Click on **Close** when you have selected all the items you want.

**9** Drag a primary key from one table to the common field (called the foreign key) in another table. This action will launch the **Edit Relationships dialogue box**, as shown in Figure 10.2.

Figure 10.2
The Edit Relationships dialogue box lets you quickly and easily update relationships between tables.

**10** Click on **Create**. Access 2007 will automatically create the relationship for the two tables – you will see a new line between the tables, indicating that the relationship has been established.

### Jargon buster

**Referential integrity** is a process that Access 2007 uses to prevent orphan records (records without relationships) and keep references synchronised so that your records don't try to access records that no longer exist. You can choose whether or not to enforce referential integrity by selecting or deselecting the option in the Edit Relationships dialogue box.

## Changing a Table Relationship

Sometimes, you will need to edit a table relationship. To do that, follow these steps.

**1** Open the database you want to create the relationships in.

**2** Click on the **Microsoft Office button**.

**3** Click on **Open**.

**4** Go to the **Database Tools tab** and click on **Relationships** in the **Show/Hide group**.

**5** Using your cursor, click on the line between the table relationships that you want to change. The line will appear thicker once you have selected it.

**6** When the proper line thickens, double-click on it. The **Edit Relationships dialogue box** will appear.

**Timesaver tip**

Instead of selecting lines between tables, you can open the **Edit Relationships dialogue box** by going to the **Design tab** and clicking on **Edit Relationships** in the **Tools group**.

**7** Make changes as desired. Click on **OK**.

## → Deleting a Table Relationship

Sometimes, you will need to edit a table relationship. To do that, follow these steps.

**1** Open the database you want to create the relationships in.

**2** Click on the **Microsoft Office button**.

**3** Click on **Open**.

**4** Go to the **Database Tools tab** and click on **Relationships** in the **Show/Hide group**.

**5** Using your cursor, click on the line between the table relationships that you want to change. The line will appear thicker once you have selected it.

**6** When the proper line thickens, click on it.

**7** Press **Delete** on your keyboard. If the confirmation message 'Are you sure you want to permanently delete the selected relationship from your database?' appears, click on **Yes**.

# 11

# Creating Tables

In this lesson, you will learn how to create tables in different ways, as well as how to enter and insert records, set table properties, and set primary keys.

## → Creating a New, Blank Table in an Existing Database

When you need to create a new, blank table, follow these steps.

**1** Open the database where you want to create the new table.

**2** Go to the **Create tab** and click on **Table** in the **Tables group**, as shown.

A new table will be inserted into the database. The table will be open in the **Datasheet View**.

## → Creating a Table from a Template

Table templates are very useful in Access 2007. They can be used to create the following types of tables:

■ assets

■ contacts

■ events

■ issues

■ tasks.

### Timesaver tip

Access 2007 table templates are compatible with Microsoft Windows SharePoint Service 3.0 lists of the same name.

To create a table based on a table template, follow these steps.

**1** Open the database where you want to create the new table.

**2** Go to the **Create tab** and click on **Table Templates** in the **Tables group**.

**3** Select a template from the list provided. A new table will be inserted into the database, although it might take several seconds. The table will be open in the **Datasheet View**.

## → Creating a Table with Links or Imported Information

There might be occasions when you want to import or link to information in an Excel worksheet, another Access database, or other sources.

**Jargon buster**

**Imported information** In Access 2007, when you import information from another program, you are actually creating a copy of the information in a new table in your database.

To create a table by importing or linking to external data, follow these steps.

**1** Open the database where you want to create the new table.

**2** Go to the **External Data tab** and click on the **data source** you desire in the **Import group**, as shown.

**3** Follow the instructions in the dialogue box provided for the data source selection you made. Access 2007 will create the new table and display it in the Navigation pane.

### Jargon buster

**Linked information** When you use a database to link to information, you are actually creating a linked table in the current database that represents a live link to the existing information that is stored somewhere else.

## → Entering Data into a Table

In Chapter 3, you learned that records in Access 2007 are really just the rows in a table. When you open a table in the Datasheet View, you can type or paste information into each record. By default, Access 2007 only accepts a specific type of data, such as text or numbers. You will see an error message if you attempt to enter information that is not valid.

To enter data into a table, follow these steps.

**1** Double-click on the **table** that you want to use in the **Navigation pane**. The table will open in the **Datasheet View** by default.

**2** Click on the first **field** that you want to use within the table.

**3** Enter your **date**.

**4** Press the **tab button** on your keyboard to move to the next field in the same record. You can also use the **right or left arrow keys** on your keyboard.

## Timesaver tip

Access 2007 commits changes to a table when the cursor moves to a new field in the same record or to another row. You don't need to continually save your data.

# → Setting Table Properties

To set table properties that apply to an entire table and/or to entire records, follow these steps.

**1** Go to the **Navigation pane** and select the table you want to open. Right-click on the table.

**2** Click on **Design View**. The table should appear similar to the one shown in Figure 11.1. If not, go to the **Design tab** under **Table Tools** and click on **Property Sheet**.

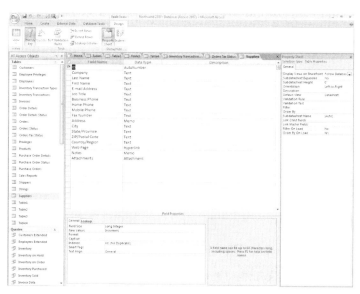

**Figure 11.1**
Opening a table in Design View allows you to set table properties quickly.

**3** In the **Property Sheet**, click on the box for the property you want to set.

**4** Type a setting for the property.

---

**Timesaver tip**

You can often click on the **ellipses button** [...] or use the dropdown arrow to select from a range in the **Property Sheet**.

---

## → Setting the Primary Key for a Table

To set a primary key for a table, follow these steps.

**1** Open the table in **Design View** by right-clicking on the table in the **Navigation pane** and selecting **Design View**.

**2** Select the field or fields that you want to use as the primary key.

**3** Go to the **Design tab** and click on **Primary Key** in the **Tools group**, as shown.

## → Removing the Primary Key for a Table

To remove a primary key for a table, follow these steps.

**1** Open the table in **Design View**.

**2** Click on the **primary key icon** in the top row of the table.

**3** Go to the **Design tab** and click on **Primary Key** in the **Tools group**. The primary key will be removed.

## Important

Access 2007 will prompt you to create a primary key if you save a new table without one. If you select **Yes**, Access will create an ID field using an AutoNumber data type. If the table already has an AutoNumber field, Access will use that as the primary key.

11

# 12

# Copying or Exporting Table Data

In this lesson, you will learn how to copy data from another source into your table. You will also discover how to export a table to a SharePoint site.

## → Copying Data from Another Source into Your Table

There will be times when you don't want to import information from another source, but you do want to include some of that source's information in your table. In that case, you will want to copy the data from the external source.

To copy information and place it in your table, follow these steps.

**1** Open the destination table in your Access 2007 database. Select the location for the new information.

**2** Open the source file that holds the information you want to copy.

**3** In the source file, select the information to copy. Press **CTRL + C** on the keyboard.

**4** In the destination table in Access, select the **row** and/or **field** where you want to place the information. Press **CTRL + V**.

## → Exporting a Table to a SharePoint Site

### Important

You cannot export a form or report to a SharePoint site even though you can export a table or a query. Instead, publish the entire database to the SharePoint site following the steps outlined in Chapter 7.

Sometimes a table from your Access database will need to be made available on a SharePoint site (this was discussed in more detail in Chapter 7).

To export a table to a SharePoint site, follow these steps.

**1** Open the Access database table that contains the information you want to export.

**2** Go to the **External Data tab** in the **Export group**. Click on **SharePoint List**, as shown. *Careful*: a similar option exists in the **Import group** as well!

**3** When the Export Wizard starts, enter the address of the SharePoint destination site in the **Specify a SharePoint site box** as shown in Figure 12.1.

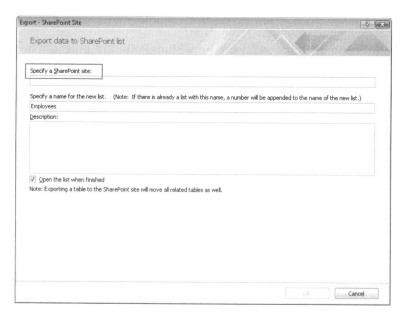

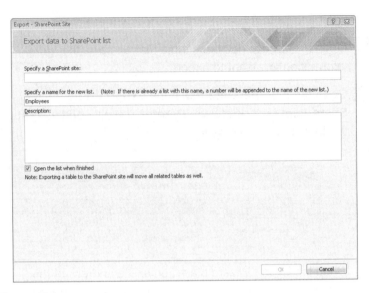

**Figure 12.1**
To export a table to a SharePoint site, you need to know the address of the site and other information.

**4** In **Specify a name for the new SharePoint list**, enter a name for the new list.

**5** If you wish, enter a description for the new list in the Description box. Select **Open the list** when finished.

**6** Click on **OK**.

**7** The export process will now begin. Access will create a list on the SharePoint site and then display the status of the process on the final page of the Wizard. When the export operation ends, close the Wizard or save your export steps as a specification.

**Timesaver tip**

Need to export a query to a SharePoint site? The steps for exporting a table to a SharePoint site are identical to the ones used for exporting a query.

# 13

# Editing Tables

In this lesson, you will learn about editing features such as adding colour, changing gridlines, changing row height, column width and font styles and sizes. You will also learn how to freeze a column and delete records.

# → Changing the Row Height

Changing the row height in a table is accomplished by using the cursor to click on a horizontal line and drag the height to where you want it. To do this, follow these steps.

**1** Select the table that you want to change.

**2** In the far left column of the table, hover your cursor over a row's horizontal line. Your cursor will change to a vertical double-ended arrow with a solid black horizontal line across the middle, as shown in Figure 13.1.

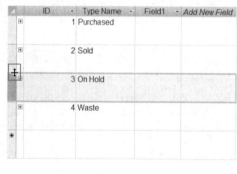

**Figure 13.1**
When changing row height, your cursor will change to a distinctive double-ended arrow with horizontal line.

**3** Click and hold the cursor as you pull the row to the desired height.

## Timesaver tip

Changing row height using the drag and drop method will apply to all rows in a table. If you prefer to change the row height to a specific numeric value, select the entire table and right-click. Click on **Row Height** and enter the numeric value you want.

# → Changing Column Width

You can use your cursor to change the width of a column in a table. Individual columns can be widened or reduced by following these steps.

**1** Select the column within a table that you want to change.

**2** In the top row of the table, hover your cursor over the column's vertical line. Your cursor will change to a vertical double-ended arrow with a solid black horizontal line across the middle, as in the example in Figure 13.1.

**3** Click and hold the cursor as you pull the column to the desired width.

**13**

## Timesaver tip

Changing column width always applies to individual columns. If you want to apply a specific numeric value to change the column width, click on the top row of the column. Right-click and select **Column Width**. Enter the numeric value you desire.

## → Changing Font Style and Size

To change the font style (from Arial to Times New Roman, for example) in a table, follow these steps.

**1** Select the table where you want to change the font style.

**2** Go to the **Home tab**. In the **Font group**, click on a font style in the **Font box**.

### Important

Changes to font style and size will apply to the entire table, not just a certain word or phrase.

To change the font size (from 10 to 16 point, for example) in a table, follow these steps.

**1** Select the table where you want to change the font size.

**2** Go to the **Home tab**. In the **Font group**, click on a font style in the **Font box**.

## → Freezing a Column

If you need to keep a certain table column in place on the left while you scroll to another position in a datasheet, you will want to freeze the column. To do that, follow these steps.

**1** Select the column(s) you want to freeze. Multiple columns are selected by holding down the **shift key** on your keyboard and clicking on additional column headers.

**2** Right-click on the column header.

**3** Click on **Freeze Columns** on the **shortcut menu**, as shown. To *unfreeze* a column, right-click on any column header, then click on **Unfreeze All Columns**.

**13**

## Timesaver tip

Frozen columns will move to the left of all other columns. To return a column to its original position in the table, you must first unfreeze it, then drag it to the location you want.

## → Changing the Look and Feel of Your Table

You can change how a table looks by making simple adjustments to the background colour and/or gridlines. To change the background colour, follow these steps.

**1** Select the table.

**2** Go to the **Home tab** and click on the **Fill/Back Color** icon, as shown.

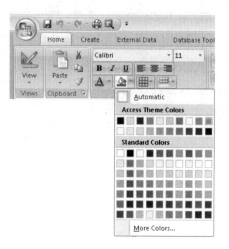

**3** Select the background colour you want from the choices provided.

To change the gridline style, follow these steps.

**1** Select the table.

**2** Go to the **Home tab** and click on the **Gridlines** icon, as shown.

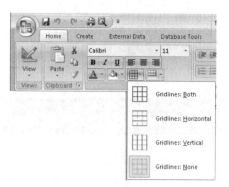

**3** Select the gridline style you prefer.

# → Deleting Records

If you need to delete a record, first determine whether or not the record is related to any other records. If a record is not related to other records, you can delete it by following these steps.

**1** Select the record.

**2** Right-click and select Delete Record.

## Timesaver tip

You can delete unrelated records by selecting them and pressing the **delete key** on your keyboard.

If a record *is* related to other records, you can still delete it. However, you will need to delete the records related to it first. If you attempt to delete a related record, an error message will appear. Click on **Help** on the error message for information about deleting the record involved.

## Important

If you delete a related record, you can also delete some or all of the records associated with the table relationship. Before deleting any related records, it's a good idea to review the table relationships and then make a backup or a copy of your database. That way you can always reverse the change if necessary.

**13**

# 14

## Saving, Closing or Deleting a Table

In this lesson, you will learn how to save, close or delete a table.

## → Saving a Table

When you add fields to a table, it's a good idea to save the table after each new one has been added – just in case! The first time you save a table, be sure to name it something that is descriptive and memorable. Databases have a lot of tables, so 'Table A' won't mean much to you after a while, but 'Product Descriptions' will remind you exactly what that table is and why you created it. You can use as many as 64 characters (this includes letters, numbers and spaces), so get as creative as you like.

To save a table, follow these steps.

**1** Click on the **Microsoft Office button**.

**2** Click on **Save**.

**3** In the **Save As dialogue box**, type a name for the table, as shown.

**4** Click on **OK**. The new name for your table will appear on the document tab just above the table.

### Timesaver tip

You can also save a table by right-clicking on the **document tab** for the table. Click on **Save** on the shortcut menu or click on the **Save icon** on the Quick Access Toolbar – that brings up the shortcut menu as well.

# → Closing a Table

When you need to close a table, just follow these steps.

**1** Right-click on the **document tab** for the table.

**2** Click on **Close** on the shortcut menu.

## Timesaver tip

Need to close all the tables that you have open? Right-click on any table's **document tab** and click on **Close All**. Careful, though – this will clear *all* open objects, not just tables. The Navigation pane will remain open, however.

# → Deleting a Table

You might need to delete a specific table from time to time. To do that, follow these steps.

**1** In the **Navigation pane**, right-click on the table you want to delete.

**2** Click on **Delete** in the shortcut menu, as shown in Figure 14.1.

**14**

**3** A message will appear, asking you to confirm your intent to delete the table. Click on **Yes**.

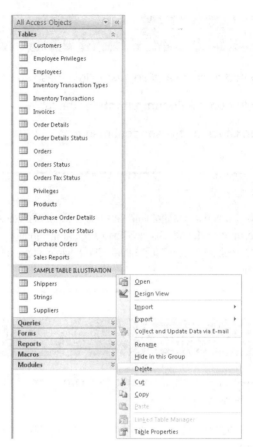

**Figure 14.1**
A shortcut menu appears when you right-click on a table in the Navigation pane.

# 15

# Using Fields in a Table

In this lesson, you will learn how to work with fields in a table, including new and existing fields, and how to set field properties. Remember, fields are also called *columns*.

## → Inserting a New Field into a New Table

Information that you want to track is stored in *fields* in a table. Remember the supporting subjects discussed in Chapter 10? Fields are typically where supporting subjects are located.

When a new table is created, it opens in the **Datasheet View**. A new field can easily be added to a new table by following these steps.

**1** In the new table, type your data in below the **Add New Field** header.

**2** Press **ENTER** on your keyboard.

A new field will automatically appear next to the field you were just typing in. New rows (records) will also be added automatically.

### Timesaver tip

As data is entered into new fields, Access analyses the information and applies a data type to the field. For example, if you enter a date in the new field, Access will recognise that information and set the data type for the field to Date/Time. As you type in the next record for that field, a calendar will automatically appear to help you with any other dates. When Access doesn't recognise what you've typed, the data type is set to Text.

## → Inserting a New field into an Existing Table

If you need a new field in an existing table, follow these steps.

**1** Double-click on the table in the **Navigation pane** to open it.

**2** Type your data into the cell below the header **Add New Field**.

**3** Press **ENTER** on the keyboard to add another new field.

# → Adding an Existing Field into a Table

When you work with a database that contains multiple tables, you can save time by adding a field from another table into the table you are currently working on. You can do this by following these steps.

**1** In the **Navigation pane**, double-click on the table that you want to add the existing field to. The table will open in the **Datasheet View**.

**2** Go to the **Datasheet tab** and click on **Add Existing Fields** in the **Fields & Columns group**, as shown.

**3** The **Field List pane** will appear. Click on the + next to a table name to see all of its available fields, as shown.

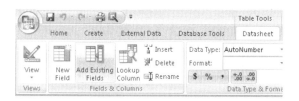

**4** When you locate the field you want to add, click on and drag the field from the **Field List pane** on to the table. A vertical yellow insertion line will appear and you can drop the field into any position where this insertion line appears, as shown.

**15**

## Important

Don't skip the Lookup Wizard. A new one-to-many relationship is automatically created between the table in the Field List pane and the table you are working with when the Lookup Wizard steps have been completed.

**5** After you have dropped the field on to the table, the Lookup Wizard will appear. Follow the prompts to complete the process.

## → Changing a Field's Content

Changing the information within a field is very simple. Follow these steps.

**1** Open the table where you want to change the information.

**2** Select the cell within the field where the information will change.

**3** Highlight the specific content that will change.

**4** Type in the new information.

## → Deleting a Field

You can delete fields easily in the Datasheet View. Follow these steps.

**1** Open the table and right-click on the field header that you want to delete.

**2** Click on **Delete Column** in the shortcut menu.

### Important

You cannot undo the deletion of a field! Before you delete a field, be certain that the information is no longer required in related tables. It's a good idea to back up the database before you delete a field or else make a separate copy of the database.

15

**3** Click on **Yes** to confirm the deletion if a confirmation message appears.

**4** Click on **Save** in the Quick Access Toolbar.

## → Moving or Copying Data in a Field

The Cut, Copy and Paste commands used in other Office applications are useful in Access 2007, too. You can use them to move or copy data in table fields. For example, maybe you want to copy a post code from one customer field into another.

To move or copy data, follow these steps.

**1** Select the cell or specific content within a field that you want to move or copy.

**2** Right-click on it.

**3** Click on **Cut** (to remove the content and place it elsewhere) or **Copy** (to copy the content and leave the original content intact).

**4** Select the new location for the content. This is usually a cell within another field.

**5** Right-click on it.

**6** Click on **Paste**.

## → Hiding or Unhiding a Field

There may be times when you don't want a specific field to be visible to everyone in the database, although you may need the content from that field. The solution is to hide the field from view so that the content remains but no one except you knows that it's there.

To hide a field, follow these steps.

**1** Right-click on the field header.

**2** Click on **Hide Columns** in the shortcut menu.

When you want the field to be visible again, follow these steps.

**1** Right-click on any field header in the applicable table.

**2** Click on **Unhide Columns** in the shortcut menu.

**3** In the **Unhide Columns dialogue box**, select the column that you want to show. The column will appear in your table as soon as you have clicked on a tick box and a tick appears in it, as shown, and you can double-check that you have selected the proper field.

**4** Click on **Close**.

**15**

Figure 15.1
Field properties can be changed in the Design View.

## Timesaver tip

Want to get to Design View quickly? Try one of these options. Right-click on the table in the **Navigation pane** and click on **Design View** in the shortcut menu or, if the table is already open, go to the **Design tab** and click on **Design** in the **Views group**.

## Jargon buster

An **input mask** controls how users enter data into a database. You can create an input mask to force people to enter phone numbers or addresses in a specific way, for example. This field property places a limit on the number of characters in a particular field and can force the use of hyphens or other characters as well.

## → Setting Field Properties

You can see the field properties for a table by opening the table in the Design View. The Field Properties pane will appear in the lower section of the window.

To set specific properties for a field, follow these steps:

**1** Select a cell within a field.

**2** In the **Field Properties pane**, select the properties that you want to change (Figure 15.1).

**3** Click on **Save**.

You can place an input mask in a table field to save time for you and help users to enter information properly.

To add an input mask to a field, follow these steps.

**1** Right-click on the table that you want to change in the **Navigation pane**.

**2** Click on **Design View** in the shortcut menu.

**3** In the **Field Properties pane**, select the **General tab**. Click on **Input Mask**.

**4** Type in the input mask. Use Access 2007 Help and Support for input mask examples if you need some guidance with this step.

**15**

**5** Click on **Save**.

# 16

# Working with Lookup Columns

In this lesson, you will learn what lookup columns are and how to work with them.

# → What is a Lookup Column?

*Lookup columns* are very useful in Access. These are fields that retrieve values from other tables or value lists. They are typically used to display a list of choices for users.

Lookup columns are created either manually (by setting a field's Lookup field properties) or automatically by using the Lookup Wizard. Either the Datasheet or Design View can be used during creation. As the Lookup Wizard is the easiest way to create a lookup column, this section will focus on using that process.

# → Lookup Field Properties

You can find lookup field properties by opening an object (usually a table or query) in Design View. The lower portion of the window will display Field Properties for the object – just click on the Lookup tab to see the properties for a lookup field.

Be sure that you have selected an actual lookup field before you look for the lookup field properties. Otherwise, you will not see anything in the properties box.

# → Creating a Lookup Column Using the Lookup Wizard

The Lookup Wizard automatically populates appropriate field properties and creates the right table relationships for you. The Lookup Wizard will start automatically in some cases, but you can start it on your own as well.

Before you begin, determine whether you want to base the lookup column on a table, a query or a list of values that you enter. For these instructions, the lookup column will be based on a table without manual entry.

To create a lookup column using the Lookup Wizard, follow these steps:

**1** Open a table in **Design View**.

> **Important**
>
> When you open a table in **Design View**, your fields will become records (rows). Don't let that confuse you; as soon as you return to **Datasheet View**, the fields will all be in column format again.

**2** In the **Data Type field**, select the record you want. Click on the **down arrow**.

**3** Click on **Lookup Wizard**. The Lookup Wizard will launch, as shown.

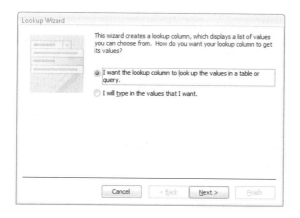

**4** Select '**I want the lookup column to look up the values in a table or query**'. Click on **Next**.

**5** Select whether you want to see Tables, Queries or Both. Click on **Next**.

**6** Drag and drop the fields containing the values you want added to your lookup column by selecting fields under **Available Fields** and using the horizontal arrows to move each field to **Selected Fields**. When you have finished choosing fields, click on **Next**.

**7** Decide how you want to sort the records. Click on **Next**.

**8** Decide how wide you want the columns to be. In this step, you can physically size the columns using your cursor. Click on **Next**.

**9** Type in a label for your lookup column. Click on **Finish**.

If prompted to save the table, click on **Yes**.

## → Changing a Lookup Column

If you need to change a lookup column, you just open the table in Design View and modify the Lookup field properties. Here's how to do that.

**1** Open the table in **Design View**.

**2** In the **Field Properties pane**, click on the **Lookup tab**.

**3** Click on the item in the right-hand column that you want to modify, as shown in Figure 16.1.

**4** If the item can be modified, a dropdown arrow or ellipses button will be visible. Use the arrow or button to make your change.

**Figure 16.1**
Lookup field properties are shown in the Design View under the
Lookup tab in Field Properties.

**5** When finished, go to the **Design tab** and click on **Datasheet
View** in the **Views group**. If prompted to save the table, click
on **Yes**.

## Timesaver tip

If a lookup column is based on a value list with Allow List Edits set to
**Yes**, you can edit list items in Datasheet or Form View.

16

# → Changing a Field to a Lookup Column

To change an existing field into a lookup column, follow these steps.

**1** Open the table in **Design View**.

**2** Select the field that you want to change.

**3** Click on the corresponding cell in the **Data Type** column. Using the drop-down arrow, click on **Lookup Wizard**.

**4** Follow the Wizard's prompts to complete the change.

# 17

# Using Forms

In this lesson, you will learn what forms are, how to use the Form Wizard and how to enter data into a form.

# → Understanding Forms

When you work with *forms*, it's important to understand that they are simply a database object used to enter, edit or display data from a table or query. Forms are used when you want to control access to data.

For example, perhaps you only want others to see certain fields or records in a table. A form can do that for you by allowing you to show users only specific fields and records and hide all the rest. Forms can include buttons and other functions to automate frequently performed actions and make it easier for people to use the database and provide accurate information. A sample form is shown in Figure 17.1.

Purchase Order Details |

| | |
|---|---|
| Product | Northwind Traders Chai ▼ |
| Quantity | 40 |
| Unit Cost | $14.00 |

**Figure 17.1**
A sample form created using the Form Wizard.

# → The Form Wizard

You can always manually create a form, but as the Form Wizard makes the process so easy, this section will focus on that. Manual form-creation methods are explained in Chapter 18.

To create a form using the Form Wizard, follow these steps.

**1** Open the table or query that will be the foundation for the form.

**2** Go to the **Create tab** and click on **More Forms** in the **Forms group**.

**3** Click on **Form Wizard**, as shown.

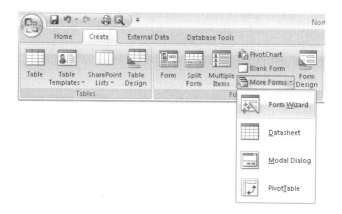

**4** In the Form Wizard, drag and drop the items in **Available Fields** you want into **Selected Fields** using the horizontal arrows, as shown.

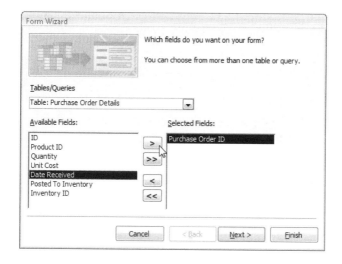

**5** Click on **Next**.

**6** Choose a layout for the form. Click on **Next**.

**7** Choose a style for the form. Click on **Next**.

**8** Type in a title for the form.

**9** Select **Open the form** to view or enter information or **Modify** to change the form's design.

**10** Click on **Finish**. The form will appear on your screen.

---

### Timesaver tip

At the bottom of a form is a **Record** section. You can use the horizontal arrows in that section to move quickly through records in the form.

---

## → Entering Data into a Form

Because forms are designed with simplicity in mind, it's very easy to enter data. Just open the form and use the button on your keyboard to move between data entry boxes. Enter the new information.

---

### Jargon buster

The **Design View** provides a detailed view of the structure of your form. For example, you can see Header, Detail and Footer sections. The form is not actually running in this view, however, so you can't see the underlying data used by the form.

# 18

# Creating Forms

In this lesson, you will learn how to create forms in Access using several different methods.

## → Creating a Form Using the Form Tool

You can create a form with a single click by using the *Form tool*. This tool pulls all fields from all underlying data sources and places them in the form.

To create a form using the Form tool, follow these steps.

**1** In the **Navigation pane**, click on the table or query that you want to use as the basis of the form.

**2** Go to the **Create tab** and click on **Form** in the **Forms group**. The process could take several seconds, but the form will appear on your screen shortly. If you need to modify the form, open it in the **Layout** or **Design View** to make changes.

### Jargon buster

The **layout view** can be used for almost any change you need to make to a form. In this view, the form is actually running. That means you can see the data even while you modify the form.

## → Creating a Form Using the Split Form Tool

*Split forms* are a new feature in Access 2007. They are single forms that provide a dual view of your data: the Form View and a Datasheet View. The two views are synchronised, so selecting a field in one area of the form selects the same field in the other part of the form. Data from either part of the form can be added, edited or deleted.

Split forms are useful because, for example, you can use one part of the form (a datasheet, for instance) to locate a record and then use the Form View to edit that record.

## Jargon buster

**Controls** are objects (a tick box is a good example) that display data, perform actions and allow you to label and place images in your form. The most commonly used control is the text box but many others are available.

To create a new split form using the Split form tool, follow these steps.

**1** In the **Navigation pane**, click on the table or query that you want to use.

**2** Go to the **Create tab** and click on **Split Form** in the **Forms group**. The process might take several seconds, but the end result on your screen should be something similar to that shown in Figure 18.1.

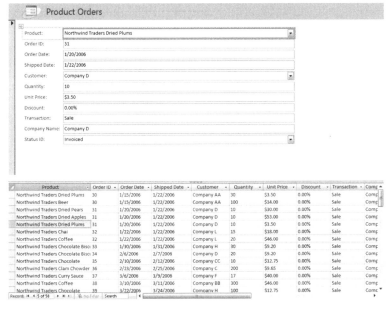

Figure 18.1
A split form created in Access.

## → Turning an Existing Form into a Split Form

If you have already created a form that you would like to now display in split form format, follow these steps.

**1** Open the existing form in the **Design View**.

**2** Click on the form and press **F4** to display the Property Sheet if it is not already displayed.

**3** Click on the down arrow at the top of the **Property Sheet** and select **Form**, as shown.

**4** Click on the **Format tab**. Select **Split Form** from the **Default View list**.

**5** Go to the **Design tab** on the **Ribbon** and click on **Form View** in the **Views group**.

### Timesaver tip

View buttons are located at the bottom right corner of a database. Just click on the button for the view you want to instantly change to that view.

# → Creating a Form with the Blank Form Tool

If you just want to put a few fields into a form, you might want to use the Blank Form process. It's fast and simple. Follow these steps.

**1** From anywhere within an open database, go to the **Create tab** and click on **Blank Forms** in the **Forms group**.

**2** A blank form will appear. The **Field List pane** will be located to its right. Click on **Show all tables** in the **Field List pane** if no fields are available for viewing.

 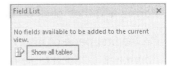

**3** Click on the plus sign (+) next to the items that contain fields you want on your form. This will expand each table so that you can see every available field.

**4** Add fields to your form by double-clicking on a field or dragging it on to the form.

> **Timesaver tip**
>
> Add a wide variety of controls to any form by switching to the **Design View** and using the **Controls group** on the **Design tab**, as shown in Figure 18.2.

**Figure 18.2**
The Controls group on the Design tab offers a variety of options for your form.

18

# → Creating a Form that Contains a Subform

*Subforms* allow you to view data from more than one table or query on the same form. They are really just forms inserted into other forms. The *primary form* is called the *main form*, the form within that the subform. These are ideal to use when you need to show data from a table or query that has a one-to-many relationship.

The easiest way to create a form containing a subform is to use the Form Wizard. Follow these steps.

**1** On the **Create tab**, in the **Forms group**, click on **More Forms** and then click on **Form Wizard**.

**2** On the first page of the Wizard, in the **Tables/Queries drop-down list**, select a table or query. For example, to create a Categories form that displays products for each category in a subform, select Table: Categories (the 'one' side of the one-to-many relationship).

**3** Double-click on the fields that you want to include from this table or query.

**4** On the same page of the Wizard, in the **Tables/Queries drop-down list**, select another table or query from the list. For example, select the Products table (the 'many' side of the one-to-many relationship).

**5** Double-click on the fields that you want to include from this table or query. Click on **Next**.

**6** Assuming that you set up the relationships correctly before starting the Wizard, the Wizard will ask '**How do you want to view your data?**' – that is, by which table or query. For example, to create the Categories form, click on by Categories. The Wizard will display a small diagram of the form. The box in the lower portion of the form represents the subform.

**7** At the bottom of the Wizard page, select the **Form with subform(s)** option.

**8** Click on **Next**.

**9** Click on **Tabular** or **Datasheet**, depending on which layout you want for your subform.

**10** Click on **Next**.

> **Timesaver tip**
>
> Both the Tabular and Datasheet layout styles arrange the subform data in rows and columns, but a tabular layout is more customisable because colour, graphics and other formatting elements can be added to it.

**11** Now, select a formatting style for the form. If you chose **Tabular** on the previous page, the formatting style you choose will also be applied to the subform. Click on **Next**.

**12** Type the titles you want for the forms. Access will title the forms based on what you type here and label the subform based on the title you type for the subform. You can also specify whether or not you want the form opened in the Form or Design View.

**13** Click on **Finish**.

> **Timesaver tip**
>
> Use the **Controls group** on the **Format tab** to add a title, page number or date and time to a form.

**18**

# → Adding a Logo to Your Form

If you would like to display your company logo on an Access form, follow these steps.

**1** Open the form in the **Layout View** (right-click on the form in the **Navigation pane** and click on **Layout View** in the shortcut menu).

**2** Go to the **Format tab** and click on **Logo** in the **Controls group**.

**3** In the **Insert Picture dialogue box**, locate the logo file and double-click on it. The logo will be added to the form. If you don't like where Access places it, just click and drag it to the location you prefer.

### Timesaver tip

You can resize a logo by placing the cursor at the edge of the logo. When the cursor changes to a double-ended arrow, drag the edge of the logo until it is the size you prefer.

# 19

# Working with Field Controls

In this lesson, you will learn what field controls are and how to work with basic controls.

# → What are Field Controls?

*Field controls* are objects that display data or perform actions. You can use these controls to improve the look and feel of a form, for example, or make it easier to use. A text box is a field control and so are labels, buttons and similar objects.

There are three types of controls to be aware of when using Access:

- **bound control** — used when the source of data is a field in a table or query

- **unbound control** — used when a source of data is not available

- **calculated control** — used when the source of data is an expression rather than a field

**Timesaver tip**

Expressions are explained in more detail in Chapter 21.

*Control layouts* – the guides that align your controls horizontally or vertically – are either *stacked* or *tabular*. You can have both kinds in a single form.

In a *stacked layout*, controls are vertical and always contained in a single section of a form. Labels for these controls are always on the left of the control.

In a *tabular layout*, the controls are arranged in rows and columns, similar to a spreadsheet. Labels are always across the top and tabular layouts cover two sections in a form.

## → Moving Field Controls

You will learn how to add field controls in Chapter 20, but it's important to know that, once you add a field control to a form, you can move it pretty much wherever you want.

To move a field control, you must be in the Design or Layout View.

Then, just select the control with your cursor. Once the cursor turns into a four-ended arrow, (like a weathervaine) drag the control to the location you prefer, as shown in Figure 19.1.

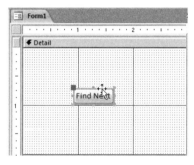

**Figure 19.1**
**Moving field controls is fast and easy in the Design or Layout View.**

If you want to position your control differently on the form, you can follow these steps.

**1** Right-click on the control.

**2** Position the cursor over **Align** or **Position** on the shortcut menu and make a selection from the corresponding menu.

## → Changing the Size of a Control

**19**

There are different ways to change the size of a control. Just like using the same kind of process that you would use to resize a text box in Word, for instance, you can select a control and then use your cursor to pull the corners or sides of the control until it is the size you prefer, as shown.

You can also follow these steps to alter the size of a control.

**1** Right-click on the control.

**2** Position the cursor over **Size** in the shortcut menu and make a selection ('To Fit', 'To Grid' and so on), as shown.

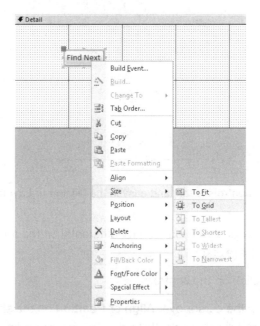

# 20

# Adding Special Controls

In this lesson, you will learn how to add a variety of special controls to forms and reports.

# → Using a Windows Visual Theme in Controls

To add a little pizzazz to your database, consider applying a Windows visual theme to the controls on your database forms. By default, Access 2007 applies Windows themes to any new databases created, although existing databases will not be automatically updated in this way. Unless you disable the use of a theme or change the display properties, each control will use that theme.

To change a Windows Vista visual theme, follow these steps.

**1** On your desktop, right-click and then click on **Personalise** in the shortcut menu, as shown.

**2** Click on **Theme** under **Personalise Appearance and Sounds**.

**3** In the **Theme Settings dialogue box**, select a new theme from the **Theme dropdown menu**, as shown.

**4** Click on **OK**.

## → Adding Text Box Controls

For most databases, the text box is the standard control used because of all the types of data that can be displayed in it. You can also use text boxes to perform calculations.

To add a text box that displays data from a field in a table or query (that is, a text box that is *bound* to an updateable record source), follow these steps.

20

**1** Open a form or report in the **Layout** or **Design View**.

**2** On the **Format tab**, click on **Add Existing Fields** in the **Controls group**.

**3** In the **Field List pane**, expand the table that holds the field you want bound to your text box.

**4** Drag the field from the **Field List pane** to the report or form.

---

### Timesaver tip

When dragging fields from the Field List pane, Access will automatically create a text box for these fields: Text, Memo, Number, Date/Time, Currency, Hyperlink.

---

To add an *unbound text box* (one that is *not* connected to a field in a table or query), follow these steps.

**1** Open a form or report in the **Design View**.

**2** On the **Design tab**, click on **Text Box** in the **Controls group**, as shown.

**3** Place your cursor where you want the text box to be located on your form or report. Drag the cursor to the approximate size for the text box. Be sure to leave a little room on the left side for the label that Access will place next to the text box.

**4** Release the cursor. The text box will be inserted.

# → Creating a List Box or Combo Box

When you place a form in your database, you're likely to be doing so to make the database easy to use. One option to consider that further enhances ease of use is the addition of a *list box* or *combo box*. These items let users select a value from a list instead of trying to remember all the available options.

List controls can connect to existing data or you can enter fixed values for the list as you create the control. Two types of list controls are available: the list box and the combo box. *List boxes* contain rows of data and usually show several rows at a time. *Combo boxes* hide the list until the down arrow is clicked. They also let you enter a value not on the list. Both types can be *bound* or *unbound controls*.

## Important

The following instructions assume that the form used is bound to a table or query. Some steps won't apply if the form is unbound. Press **F4** to bring up the form's property sheet and determine whether or not your chosen form is bound. **Record Source** in the **Data tab** of the Property Sheet will show which table or query a form is bound to.

To create a list box or combo box, follow these steps.

**1** In the **Navigation pane**, right-click on the form where you want to place the list box or combo box.

**2** Click on **Design View** in the shortcut menu.

**3** Go to the **Design tab** and verify that **Use Control Wizards** has been selected in the **Controls group**, as shown.

**20**

**4** In the **Controls group**, click on either the **List Box** ⊞ or **Combo Box** ⊞

**5** Click on the form where you want the list box or combo box to be placed. The appropriate Wizard will launch, as shown.

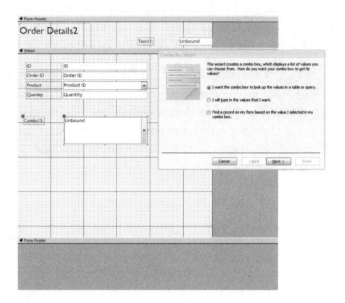

**6** The Wizard will ask how you want to obtain the values for the control.

■ Click on '**I want the list box/combo box to look up the values in a table or query**' if you want to show current data from a record source.

■ Click on '**I will type in the values that I want**' if you want to show a fixed list of values.

■ Click on '**Find a record on my form based on the value I selected in my list box/combo box**' if you want the control to perform a find operation.

**7** Follow the Wizard's prompts to specify how values will appear according to the choice you made.

**8** If you are asked what you want Access to do when you select a value:

- click on '**Remember the value for later use**' if you want to create an unbound control

- click on '**Store that value in this field**' to create a bound control.

**9** Click on **Next**.

**10** Type a label for the control.

**11** Click on **Finish**.

To see how the list box or combo box looks on your form, switch to the Form View. Figure 20.1 shows an example of a combo box created using the Wizard.

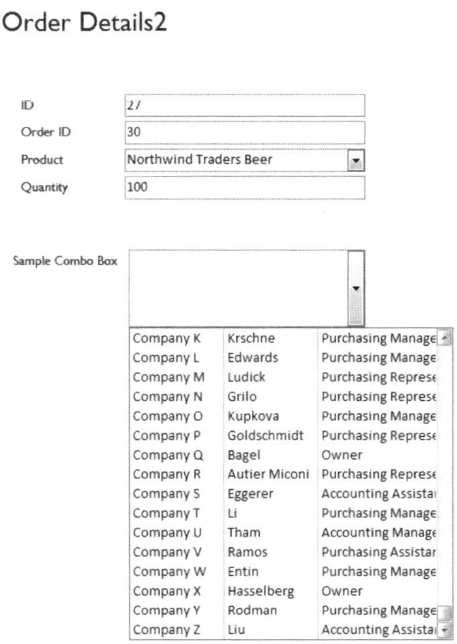

Order Details2

Figure 20.1
A combo box can help users of your database select information quickly and accurately.

# → Creating a Calculated Control

When you want to display the results of a calculation, use a *calculated control* in your form or report. For example, if you want to show the number of products sold as well as the price of each product, you can create a calculated text box that multiplies the two fields to display a total price.

> ## Timesaver tip
>
> Any control that has a Control Source property can be used as a calculated control.

To create a calculated control, follow these steps.

**1** In the **Navigation Pane**, right-click on the form or report you want to use.

**2** Click on **Design View** in the shortcut menu.

**3** Go to the **Design tab** and click on the tool you want in the **Controls group**.

**4** Click on the location in the form where you want the list control placed.

**5** If a Control Wizard launches, click **Cancel** to close it.

**6** Select the control and press **F4** to show the related property sheet. Type an expression in the **Control Source property box** on the **Data tab**. If you need help creating the expression, click on the **ellipses button**, as shown, to launch the Expression Builder (explained in more detail in Chapter 22).

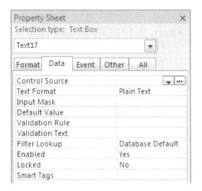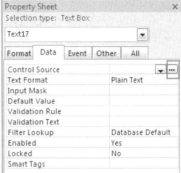

**7** Switch to **Form** or **Report view** to verify that the calculated control works as you expect.

## → Creating a Command Button

When you want a button on a form to start an action or series of actions, you need to create a *command button*. Such buttons use macros or event procedures that launch when the button is clicked on. For example, if you want a report to automatically open from a form, a command button can perform that action for you. You can create a command button in different ways, but the steps outlined here use the Command Wizard, which is very straightforward.

To create a command button, follow these steps.

**1** In the **Navigation pane**, right-click on the form.

**2** Click on **Design View** in the shortcut menu.

**3** Verify that **Use Control Wizards** is selected in the **Controls group** of the **Design tab**.

**4** In the **Controls group**, click on the **Button** icon

**5** Click on where you want the command button to be inserted into your form.

**6** Follow the prompts of the **Command Button Wizard**.

**7** Click on **Finish**.

**20**

The Wizard will create a command button and embed a macro in the button's On Click property to perform the task you selected when using the Wizard.

**Jargon buster**

The **Option group** provides various buttons or input boxes that can be used to help quickly enter information into a form. Users simply select from the options provided. Option groups can use **option buttons** (where only one response is valid), **tick boxes** (where more than one response is possible) and **toggle buttons** (where a 'yes' or 'no' is required).

## → Creating an Option Group

To create an option group, follow these steps.

**1** In the **Navigation pane**, right-click on the form you want.

**2** Click on **Design View in the shortcut menu**.

**3** Go to the **Design tab** and verify that **Use Control Wizards** is selected in the **Controls** group.

**4** Click on the **Option Group** icon ▣ in the **Controls group**.

**5** Click on the location in the form where you want the option group placed.

**6** The **Option Group Wizard** will launch. Follow the prompts.

**7** Click on **Finish**.

**Timesaver tip**

You can create option buttons by selecting the individual option button in the Controls group instead of using the Controls group process. Just click on the Option button, Check (tick) Box or Toggle button.

# → Inserting Date and Time into a Form or Report

Date and time information is useful in a variety of databases. To insert the date and time into a form or report, follow these steps.

**1** In the **Navigation pane**, right-click on the form or report.

**2** Click on **Layout View** in the shortcut menu.

**3** Go to the **Format tab** and click on **Date and Time** in the **Controls group**.

**4** To include the date, click on the date format you want to use. Otherwise, clear the **Include Date** tick box.

**5** To include the time, click on the time format you want to use. Otherwise, clear the **Include Time** tick box.

**6** Click on **OK**. The date and/or time information will be added to the form or report.

**20**

# 21

# Using Expressions

In this lesson, you will learn basic information about how expressions are used in an Access database and how to create an expression using the Expression Builder.

# → Understanding Expressions

*Expressions* are similar to the formulae used in Excel. They can:

■ perform a calculation

■ retrieve the value of a field or control

■ define rules

■ create calculated controls and fields

■ provide criteria for a query

■ define grouping levels for reports.

Expressions are typically used when you need to create a value that isn't available directly from your data. For instance, if you need to calculate the total value of an order, you would create an expression to accomplish that task because, typically, a form or report will not show that information.

There are various places in a database where an expression can be used. Tables, queries, forms, reports and macros can all accept expressions.

Use expressions when you need to accomplish any of the following in Access:

■ calculate values that don't directly exist in your data

■ set default values for table fields or controls on a form or report

■ create validation rules to control what users enter into a field or control

■ set criteria for a query.

*Expressions* reference the names of the fields in tables and queries as well as the names of controls. Field or control names in an expression are always enclosed in brackets, like these **[ ]**. The most commonly used place for an expression is in a text box control in a form or report.

# → Creating an Expression Using the Expression Builder

The Expression Builder can help you to build an expression from scratch or it will let you choose from pre-built expressions for some items.

In Figure 21.1, you can see the different sections in the Expression Builder. Section 1 shows the expression box, where expressions are constructed. Section 2 shows the operator buttons that can be used when building an expression. Section 3 comprises three columns: the left column shows the folders with the tables, queries, forms and reports in your database, along with a variety of functions; the middle column shows specific elements of the folder selected in the left column; the right column lists any values for the elements selected in the first two columns.

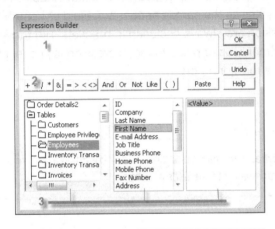

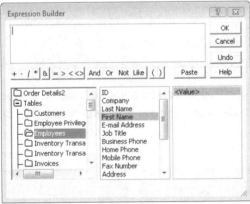

**Figure 21.1**
The Expression Builder is a useful tool for quickly building expressions in Access.

To create an expression in a table using the Expression Builder, form or report, follow these steps.

**1** Right-click on the object you want to open in the **Navigation pane**. Click on **Design View** in the shortcut menu.

**2** Open the **Expression Builder**. This can be done from anywhere you see the **Build button**, as shown in Figure 21.2. It's typically found in the **Control Source property** of a control or in the **Validation Rule property** of a table field.

**Figure 21.2**
The Expression Builder is opened with the Build button in the Property Sheet.

**3** Fill in the **Expression Builder** with the details required for your specific needs.

**Timesaver tip**

If you need more information to build a specific expression for your database, click on the **Help button** in the **Expression Builder** and search for 'Create an Expression' or 'Examples of Expressions'. The former provides a Table of Operators; the latter offers dozens of expression examples that can be copied directly into your database.

# 22

# Using Conditional Formatting

In this lesson, you will learn the basics of using conditional formatting in Access 2007, including how to apply it to a control based on its own value, use an expression to apply conditional formatting to one or more controls, change the formatting of a conditional control and remove conditional formatting.

Conditional formatting for controls is used to selectively highlight information on a form or report. For example, you might want to highlight products within a certain price range in a form or clearly identify negative numbers in a report by making them red. Conditional formatting can be set for a text box or combo box control.

# → Applying Conditional Formatting to a Control Based on its Own Value

When you want to apply conditional formatting to a control that meets specific criteria, follow these steps.

**1** In the **Navigation pane**, right-click on the form or report you want to apply the conditional formatting to.

**2** Click on **Layout View** in the shortcut menu.

**3** Click on the control that you want to apply the formatting to.

**4** Go to the **Format tab** and click on **Conditional** in the **Font group**, as shown.

**5** In the **Conditional Formatting dialogue box**, select the formatting options you want under **Default Formatting**, as shown.

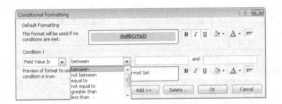

**6** Under **Condition 1**, use the down arrows to select the criteria you want for the conditional formatting.

**7** To add another conditional format for the same control, click on **Add** and repeat steps 5 and 6. When you have finished adding all the conditional formats, click on **OK**.

Order Details2

| | |
|---|---|
| ID | 28 |
| Order ID | 30 |
| Product | Northwind Traders Dried Plums ▾ |
| Quantity | *30* |

Sample Combo Box [                    ] ▾

**Figure 22.1**
In this form, the Quantity field has been highlighted as the quantity is less than 100.

In Figure 22.1, the Quantity field shows the effects of a conditional format having been applied to that field: the font and background have been highlighted as the figure is less than 100.

## Important

Conditions must be based on the lookup ID, not the value returned by the lookup field. Also, conditions are evaluated by Access and applied so that no conflicts occur. If you notice that a conditional format you created is not working correctly, it's likely that it conflicts with another conditional format you created. Go back and review all the conditions to determine which one(s) are creating conflicts.

# → Using an Expression to Apply Conditional Formatting to Controls

## Important

When using expression to apply conditional formatting, controls being formatted cannot use the same names as any of the fields in the form's or report's underlying record source. If you do, Access is unable to determine what you are referring to and cannot evaluate the expression.

To apply conditional formatting using an expression, follow these steps.

**1** In the **Navigation pane**, right-click on the form or report you want to apply conditional formatting to.

**2** Click on **Layout View** in the shortcut menu.

**3** Click on the control that you want to apply the formatting to.

**4** Go to the **Format tab** and click on **Conditional** in the **Font group**.

**5** In the **Conditional Formatting dialogue box**, select the formatting options you want under **Default Formatting**.

**6** Under **Condition 1**, select **Expression Is**.

**7** Type an expression into the box next to **Expression Is**, as shown.

> **Important**
>
> Do not precede an expression with an equals sign (=).

**8** Select the formatting options you want under **Condition 1**.

**9** If you want to add another conditional format for the control, click on **Add**. Repeat steps 5–8. You can add up to three conditional formats for a single control.

**10** When you have finished, click on **OK**.

## → Changing the Conditional Formatting of a Focus Control

In a form, a control has *focus* when the cursor is placed on it. To change the conditional formatting applied to a control that has focus, follow these steps.

**1** In the **Navigation pane**, right-click on the form containing the control you want to change.

**2** Click on **Layout View** in the shortcut menu.

**3** Click on the control that you want to apply the formatting to.

**4** Go to the **Format tab** and click on **Conditional** in the **Font group**.

**5** In the **Conditional Formatting dialogue box**, select the formatting options you want under **Default Formatting**.

**6** Under **Condition 1**, select **Field Has Focus** using the down arrow, as shown.

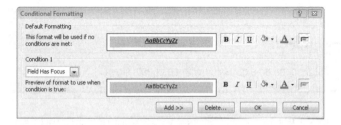

**7** Select the formatting options you want under **Condition 1** for when the control has focus.

**8** Click on **OK**.

**Important**

You can only select **Field Has Focus** under **Condition 1**. If you have applied additional conditions to a control, you will not be able to use this option for those additional conditions.

## → Removing Conditional Formatting

Removing conditional formatting is fast and easy, just follow these steps.

**1** In the **Navigation pane**, right-click on the form containing the control you want to change.

**2** Click on **Layout View** in the shortcut menu.

**3** Click on the control that will remove the formatting.

**4** Go to the **Format tab** and click on **Conditional** in the **Font group**.

**5** Click on **Delete** in the **Conditional Formatting dialogue box**.

**6** Select a tick box for each condition that you want to delete, as shown. Click on **OK**.

**7** In the **Conditional Formatting dialogue box**, click on **OK**.

## 22

# 23

# Sorting and Finding Data

In this lesson, you will learn the difference between sorting and filtering, as well as how to sort data in several different ways.

# → The Difference Between Sorting and Filtering

As you work with the information in your database, it's important to understand the difference between sorting and filtering so that you can easily find the information you need. *Sorting* organises the information you ask for and shows you all the available data. *Filtering* limits your view of the data to specific records.

For example, if you had a 200-page product list and wanted to see the products in alphabetical order, you would sort the information and still be able to see all the products. If, however, you wanted to find items in a certain portion of the alphabet, a filter would show you only those records.

When you save a table or other object with sorted data, the sort order is automatically saved along with the object. This is called *last-applied sort order*. A *default sort order* is one that is built into a query or report. It is applied when no other sort orders have been set.

### Timesaver tip

*Last-applied sort orders* can be automatically applied every time you open an object by setting the **Order By On Load** property to **Yes**. This is found in the property sheet for an object. Tables and queries show this on the **General tab** and forms and reports show it on the **Data tab**.

# → Sorting a Table, Query or Form

You can apply sorting to more than one field at a time. When you do sort for multiple fields, define the inner and outer fields. For instance, if you are applying sorting to a Customer table on the FirstName and LastName fields and want the *first names* sorted from A to Z, FirstName is the inner field. If, however, you prefer to sort by LastName and want the *last names* sorted within each first name, LastName is the inner field. Think about the way the records will be sorted first (outer) and second (inner) to help you sort accurately.

To apply sorting to a table, query or form, follow these steps.

**23**

**1** Open the object and determine the fields you want to sort in the object.

**2** Right-click on the column or corresponding control for the innermost field.

**3** Click on a sort command, as shown. What these will be will vary depending on the data in the selected field.

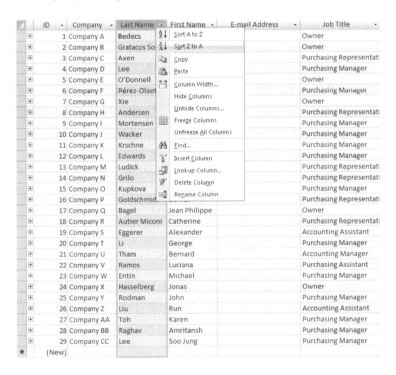

**4** Repeat these steps for each field that you want to sort. The last field selected will be the outermost field. The records will be arranged in the new sort order you have selected.

## → Sorting Records in Case-Sensitive Order

When you sort records in case-sensitive order, you are telling Access to treat lower- and upper-case letters the same. So, for example, jones and Jones will be treated as if they were exactly the same.

For this process, you will need to apply Visual Basic for Applications (VBA) code. Because writing code is beyond the scope of this book, you will need to refer to Access 2007 Help and Support for specific information about how to write the code and sort records in this manner.

## → Sorting Records in a Customised Order

Sometimes you will want to sort data in something other than alphabetical or numerical order. Perhaps you want to sort weekdays so that Sunday appears first. You can do this in the Datasheet View for tables and queries and in the Form View for a form.

Let's assume that you need to rank customers. In order to do that, you will need to create an expression during the process. For these instructions, open the Employees table in Datasheet View from the Northwind 2007 database. Then follow these steps.

**1** Go to the **Home tab** and click on **Advanced** in the **Sort & Filter group**.

**2** Click on **Advanced Filter/Sort** in the shortcut menu, as shown.

**3** The **EmployeesFilter1 tab** will open. In the lower pane, add the fields that you want by using the down arrow in the cell next to **Field**. Add **First Name** to the first cell, **Last Name** to the second cell, **Job Title** to the third, as shown.

**4** Right-click on the first available blank column in the **Field row**.

**5** Click on **Zoom** in the shortcut menu.

**6** Type in this expression: **Expr1: IIf([Job Title]="Vice President, Sales",1,IIf([Job Title]="Sales Manager",2,IIf([Job Title]="Sales Representative",3,IIf([Job Title]="Sales Coordinator",4,5))))**

**7** Click on the **Sort row** in the column containing the expression. Use the down arrow and click **Ascending**.

**8** Go to the **Home tab** and click on **Toggle Filter** in the **Sort & Filter group**. Access will return you to the original table. The new sorting criteria will be applied.

**Important**

By default, numbers are sorted based on the individual digits that make up the value, *not* their numeric value. For example, the value 11 appears before 2 and the value 12 appears before 3.

## → Sorting Records Based on Numeric Values Stored in a Text Field

There are often occasions when you will need to sort by numeric values in a text field. To do this, you will probably need to make some adjustments to the applicable field.

**Jargon buster**

There are ten separate **data types** in Access 2007. They are used to store specific types of information about a particular field. For example, if you need to store names and addresses, those fields should be set as Text data types. In comparison, a field with dates and times should be a Date/Time data type.

One way to adjust the field is to change the data type to Number from Currency. This can be done when a field contains only numeric values. To change the data type, follow these steps.

**1** Open the table in **Datasheet View**.

**2** Select the field that you want to change.

**3** Go to the **Data Type & Formatting group** on the **Datasheet tab**. Click on the arrow in the dropdown list for **Data Type** and select a new data type.

**4** Click on **Save** in the **Quick Access Toolbar**.

Otherwise, follow these steps in Datasheet View to sort records by numeric values stored in a text field.

**1** Select the field in the table that you wish to sort.

**2** Go to the **Home tab** and click on **Advanced** in the **Sort & Filter group**.

**3** Click on **Advanced Filter/Sort** in the shortcut menu.

**4** In the **Field row** of the first column in the lower pane, type the following expression, using the actual name of your field in place of '[*Fieldname*]':

> **Expr1: IIf([*Fieldname*] Is Null, 0, Val([*Fieldname*]))**

**5** In the **Sort cell**, select **Ascending** or **Descending**, as shown.

**6** Go to the **Home tab** and click on **Toggle Filter** in the **Sort & Filter group**.

**Timesaver tip**

Another way to sort numeric values without changing the structure of a table is to pad digits with leading zeros. So, instead of using the numbers 11, 2, 2000 and 3, you would change them to 0011, 0002, 2000 and 0003, then apply the sort criteria.

## → Sorting Records by Date Values

Sorting by date is a fast process – just follow these steps.

**1** Open the object containing the date field you want. Select the field.

**2** Right-click on it.

**3** Select **Sort Oldest to Newest** or **Sort Newest to Oldest**, as shown.

# 24

# Using Filters

In this lesson, you will learn how to work with filters in Access 2007. There are many ways to use filters and this chapter will give you the foundation you need to get started.

# → Understanding Filters

*Filters* simply change the way in which a form or report displays data. The design of the form or report doesn't change. A filter essentially identifies the field values you want to see so that only the records you want to see are shown. All the rest are hidden until the filter is removed.

In Access 2007, common filters are built into every view that displays data, including the Layout view. The actual filter commands available will depend on the type of field and the values within it. To access the filter commands, follow these steps.

**1** Select the field you want to filter.

**2** On the **Home tab**, click on **Filter** in the **Sort & Filter group**.

**3** Select the filtering options you want from the menu(s) provided.

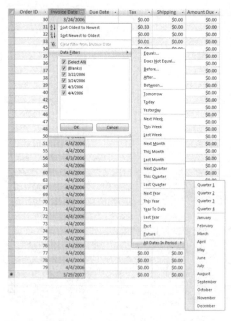

**Figure 24.1**
An example of the common kinds of filters applied to a date field.

## Important

Only a single filter is in effect for a field at any given time. When you apply a filter to a column that has already had a filter applied to it, the previous filter is removed in favour of the new filter.

# → Filtering Table Data by Selection

If a value you want to use in a filter is already being used, you can still filter the view by using a *Selection command*.

To filter based on selection, follow these steps.

**1** Go to the **Home tab** and click on **Selection** in the **Sort & Filter group**, as shown.

**2** Choose a **Selection command** from the menu.

# → Applying Advanced Filters

There may be times when you want to apply a filter that is not in the common filters list. In such cases, you will want to apply an advanced filter. To do that, follow these steps.

**1** Open a query, table, form or report in the **Datasheet**, **Form**, **Report** or **Layout View**.

**2** Verify that the view is not already being filtered. To do this, go to the **Home tab** and click on **Advanced** in the **Sort & Filter**

**group**. Click on **Clear All Filters**. If that option is dimmed, no filters are in effect.

**3** On the **Home tab**, click on **Advanced** in the **Sort & Filter group**.

**4** Click on **Advanced Filter/Sort**, as shown. This action opens a filter document tab for the object that you want to filter.

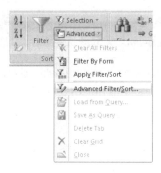

**5** In the lower pane, add the fields to the grid that you want to include in the filter by using the down arrow for the **Field row** in each column.

**6** In the **Criteria row**, specify a criterion for each field.

**7** On the **Home tab**, click on **Toggle Filter** in the **Sort & Filter group**.

## Timesaver tip

When you're on a filter document tab, right-click anywhere above the design grid. This will launch a shortcut menu that offers the commands Apply Filter/Sort, Clear Grid, Load from Query, Save As Query and Close.

## → Saving Filters as Queries

If you want to save a specific filter as a query, follow these steps.

**1** On the **Filter tab**, right-click anywhere above the grid.

**2** Select **Save As Query** in the shortcut menu, as shown.

| | |
|---|---|
| Y | Apply Filter/Sort |
| ✕ | Clear Grid |
| | Load from Query... |
| | Save As Query |
| | Close |

**3** Name the query in the **Save As Query dialogue box**.

**4** Click on **OK**. The query will now appear in the **Navigation pane** and show the results of the applied filter.

### Timesaver tip

You can clear a single filter from a single field by right-clicking on the filtered column or control. Click on **Clear Filter from [Fieldname]**. To clear multiple fields of filters, go to the **Home tab** and click on **Advanced** in the **Sort & Filter group**. Click on **Clear All Filters**.

### Important

A *criterion* is also known as an *expression* in Access 2007. For filtering purposes, criteria can be very simple (for example, >25 and <50) and are typically applied by data type. For specific lists of criteria by data type, search for "Examples of query criteria" in Access Help and Support.

# 25

# Reporting Fundamentals

In this lesson, you will learn about the elements of a report, how to choose record sources for your report and use totals, averages, percentages or running sums in your reports.

# → Understanding Report Sections

Every Access report is divided into *sections*. The sections will vary depending on the report, but include report, page and group headers, details, as well as group, page and report footers.

The *report header* shows at the beginning of a report, while the *page header* is shown at the top of every page. *Group headers* are shown at the beginnings of new groups of records. The *details section* includes information from every row in the record source and is used to hold the controls that make up the main portion of the report.

The *report footer* is printed at the end of the report and the *group footer* at the end of each record group, while the *page footer* appears at the end of each page.

As you create a report, add bound controls first and then add any unbound or calculated controls. It's easiest to work on a report in Layout View – you can quickly adjust the report format, add new fields and set properties for the report and its controls there.

# → Choosing Record Sources for Your Report

Access reports pull information from tables or queries and the object used for the underlying data is called a report's *record source*.

If a single table holds all the fields you want to use in your report, you can use that *table* as the record source. However, if you need to use fields from multiple tables, you will need to use a *query* (one or more) as the record source.

When you use a query as a record source for a report, you can do it in different ways. You can use the Report Wizard, manual steps to set the Record Source property to a query in a report's Design View or manual steps to create a new query by using the Build button in a report's Design View.

## → Using Totals, Averages, Percentages or Running Sums in Reports

To help make your data more understandable for readers, it's a good idea to use totals, averages, percentages and/or running sums in your reports. This makes it easier for them to find information and comprehend a report.

If you want to add a total or average to a report, follow these steps, in Layout View.

**1** Right-click on the report (the steps used to create a report are given in Chapter 26) in the **Navigation pane.**

**2** Click on **Layout View.**

**3** Click on the field that you want to summarise.

**4** Go to the **Format tab** and click on **Totals** in the **Grouping & Totals group.**

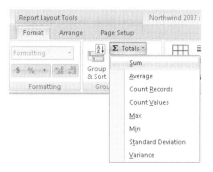

**5** Click on the aggregate type that you want to use in the field (sum, average and so on), as shown. In the report footer section, the calculation that you want will be displayed, as shown in Figure 25.1, where the average for the field was requested.

| | | | | | |
|---|---|---|---|---|---|
| Northwind Traders Syrup | $0.00 | $500.00 | $0.00 | $0.00 | $500.00 |
| Northwind Traders Long Grain Rice | $0.00 | $280.00 | $0.00 | $0.00 | $280.00 |
| Northwind Traders Chai | $270.00 | $0.00 | $0.00 | $0.00 | $270.00 |
| Northwind Traders Almonds | $0.00 | $200.00 | $0.00 | $0.00 | $200.00 |
| Northwind Traders Scones | $0.00 | $200.00 | $0.00 | $0.00 | $200.00 |
| Northwind Traders Dried Plums | $140.00 | $52.50 | $0.00 | $0.00 | $192.50 |
| | $22,992.50 | $29,070.25 | $0.00 | $0.00 | $52,062.75 |
| | | $1,263.92 | | | |
| | | | | | |
| Northwind Traders Chai | $270.00 | $0.00 | $0.00 | $0.00 | $270.00 |
| Northwind Traders Almonds | $0.00 | $200.00 | $0.00 | $0.00 | $200.00 |
| Northwind Traders Scones | $0.00 | $200.00 | $0.00 | $0.00 | $200.00 |
| Northwind Traders Dried Plums | $140.00 | $52.50 | $0.00 | $0.00 | $192.50 |
| | $22,992.50 | $29,070.25 | $0.00 | $0.00 | $52,062.75 |
| | | $1,263.92 | | | |

**Figure 25.1**
Totals are shown in the report footer section.

To calculate a percentage value and add it to a report, follow these steps.

**1** Right-click on the report you want in the **Navigation pane**.

**2** Click on **Design View** in the shortcut menu.

**3** If your report does not calculate group totals, click on the **Group footer section** and add a text box.

**4** If your report does not calculate a grand total, click on the **Report footer section** and add a text box, as shown.

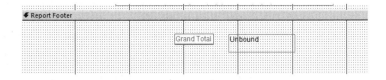

**5** If you want to calculate the percentage of each item in relation to a group or grand total, add a text box to the **Detail section**.

**6** If you want to calculate the percentage of a group of items in relation to the grand total, add a text box to the **Group header or footer** section.

**7** Select a text box. Press **F4** to display the **Property Sheet** if it is not visible.

**8** Click on the **Data tab** in the **Property Sheet**.

**9** Type an expression into the **Control Source** property box that divides the smaller total by the larger total (be sure that the smaller total is part of the larger total). For example, [DailyTotal]/[GrandTotal] (if you need help with this, click on the **ellipses button** to launch the **Expression Builder**).

**25**

**10** Set the **Format property** of the text box to **Percent**. Switch to the **Layout View** to see the results.

To calculate a running sum and add it to a report, follow these steps.

**1** Right-click on the report you want in the **Navigation pane**.

**2** Click on **Design View** in the shortcut menu.

**3** Create a text box in the **Detail**, **Group header** or **Group footer section**. Delete any label that appears or change the label text to reflect the running sum.

**4** Select the text box. Press **F4** to display the Property Sheet if it is not already visible.

**5** In the **Property Sheet**, click on the **Data tab**.

**6** In the **Control Source property box**, type in the field name or the expression for the running sum.

**7** Click on the **Running Sum property box**.

**8** Using the dropdown arrow, select **Over Group** if you want the running sum to reset to zero when the next higher grouping is reached *or* select **Over All** if you want the running sum to accumulate until the end of the report.

**9** Close the Property Sheet. Go to the **Layout View** to see the results.

# 26

# Creating a Report

In this lesson, you will learn how to create different types of reports in Access 2007. Because reports can vary wildly, based on individual requirements, it's a good idea to determine which fields, tables and queries contain the data needed for a report before creating it.

# → Creating a Report Using the Report Wizard

The Report Wizard is a useful tool because it lets you be very selective about the fields that appear in your report. To create a report using the Report Wizard, follow these steps.

**1** Go to the **Create tab** and click on **Report Wizard** in the **Reports group**, as shown.

**2** Decide which fields you want in your report by selecting the table or query record source(s) and moving available fields to selected fields by using the horizontal arrows.

**3** Click on **Next**.

**4** Add grouping levels as desired by using the horizontal arrows to add the levels and the vertical arrows to move the groups to their proper positions, as shown. See under "Creating a grouped or summary report" later in this chapter for more information about grouping.

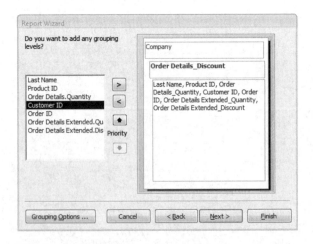

**5** Click on **Next**.

**6** Choose the sort order and summary information for the detail records.

**7** Click on **Next**.

**8** Select the layout and orientation for the report.

**9** Click on **Next**.

**10** Select the style for the report.

**11** Click on **Next**.

**26**

**12** Title the report. Select **Preview the Report** if it has not already been selected.

**13** Click on **Finish**.

---

**!**

## Important

To include fields from multiple tables and queries when using the Report Wizard, simply continue to select record sources and/or fields before you click on Next or Finish in a particular page of the Wizard.

---

## → Creating a Report Using the Report Tool

The *Report tool* is probably the quickest way to create a report because it is generated immediately without any information from you. Instead, the Report tool uses all the underlying information from the record source to create a report. However, this method does not usually result in a fine-tuned report – you will need to make some design and layout adjustments in most cases.

To create a report using the Report tool, follow these steps.

**1** Go to the **Navigation pane** and click on the table or query that the report will be based on.

**2** Go to the **Create tab** and click on **Report** in the **Reports group**.

**Timesaver tip**

Each time you save and close a report created using the Report tool, close its record source, too. Then, the next time you open the report, you will see the most recent data from the record source.

# → Creating a Report Using the Blank Report Tool

When you want to build a report from scratch, use the *Blank Report tool*. This method is perfect for reports that just require a few fields.

To create a report using the Blank Report tool, follow these steps.

**1** On the **Create tab**, click on **Blank Report** in the **Reports group**, as shown.

**2** A blank report will appear in **Layout View**. In the **Field List pane**, click on the plus sign (+) to see all the fields available for the report. If you don't see any fields, click on **Show All Tables**.

**3** Click on and drag the fields you want on to the report.

**4** To add details such as title, page numbers and so on, go to the **Format tab** and use the tools in the **Controls group**.

# → Creating and Using Subreports

When you create a report, you can also create a subreport. Essentially, this is a method for combining reports. The *primary report* is that containing the subreport. The primary report can be either bound or unbound.

## Timesaver tip

To add a subreport quickly, open the primary report in **Design View** and then drag a table, query, form or another report from the **Navigation pane** into the primary report. If Access can't figure out how to link the two objects, it will launch the Subreport Wizard. Just follow the prompts to complete the process.

To create a subreport using the Subreport Wizard, follow these steps.

**1** Open the primary report in the **Design View**.

**2** Go to the **Design tab** and verify that **Use Control Wizards** has been selected in the **Controls group**.

**3** Click on the **Subform/Subreport icon** in the **Controls group**.

**4** In the primary report, click on the location where the subreport is to go.

**5** In the Wizard, decide which data you want to use for your subreport. Click on **Next**.

**6** Choose the fields for the subreport. Click on **Next**.

**7** Decide how you want to define the fields. Click on **Next**.

**8** Type in a name for the subreport.

**9** Click on **Finish**. Switch to **Report View** to see how the subreport appears within your report, as shown. Make adjustments as desired.

Monthly Sales Report                        Thursday, March 29, 2007     10:41:13 AM

June, 2006

Product                                                        Sales
Northwind Traders Boysenberry Spread                        $2,250.00

                                    Customers subreport
                                    Company            E-mail Address              Last Name

Northwind Traders Dried Apples                              $1,590.00

                                    Customers subreport
                                    Company            E-mail Address              Last Name

## Jargon buster

The **group interval** determines how records are grouped together. For example, you can group information by day or week or letter of the alphabet. Each of such group is a group interval.

# → Creating a Grouped or Summary Report

Dividing information into groups or summaries in a report is very helpful to readers. In Access, a *group* is a collection of records that can be separated visually to display different information for each group. For example, you may decide to group information by date or sales representative.

When using the Report Wizard to include more than one table in a report, you will be asked if you want to add any grouping levels. On that page of the Wizard, there is a button called Grouping Options.

When you click on the Grouping Options button, a new dialogue box will appear with the option to select specific grouping intervals. With these, you can customise how records are grouped in your report. The choices provided will be appropriate to the corresponding field type.

26

# 27

# Saving or Editing a Report

In this lesson, you will learn how to save and edit reports.

## Important

Save early and save often! You can save a report very easily by using the **Save** button on the **Quick Access Toolbar** or by pressing **CTRL + S** for a fast save from the keyboard. You will also be prompted to save a report whenever changes have been made and if **Close** is selected before the changes have been saved.

# → Modifying Your Report in the Layout View

The Layout View can be used for almost any change you need to make to a report. The report is actually running when you're in this view, which means that you can see the data in pretty much the same form that it will be in when the report is printed. It won't be exactly the same, however – page breaks and columns won't be displayed exactly like they will when printed, but you can still see the information.

In this view, you can change column and field widths, row or field height, the formatting of a field, bind text boxes to a different field and more. This chapter will provide some examples of how reports can be modified in the Layout View. As you practise these steps, take time to notice the other commands in the various command groups, such as page numbers and date and time.

To change the page setup, follow these steps.

**1** Open the report in the **Layout View**. Click on the **Page Setup tab**, as shown.

**2** In the **Page Layout group**, there are several options to choose from:

■ click on **Size** to change the paper size

■ click on **Portrait or Landscape** to change the orientation of the report for printing and viewing

■ click on **Margins** to adjust margins within the report

■ click on **Columns** to adjust the size and number of columns in the report.

**Timesaver tip**

To quickly add a bound text box to a report, click on and drag the field from the **Field List pane** on to the report. Access will automatically create a text box for the field. This quick step can be used for text, memo, number, date/time, currency and hyperlink fields.

To change the formatting within a field, follow these steps.

**1** Open the report in the **Layout View**.

**2** Select the field you want to format. Click on the **Format tab**.

**3** Use the **Font group tools** to make changes to the font and apply other formatting to the field, as shown.

To wrap text within a field, follow these steps.

**1** Open the report in the **Layout View**.

**2** Right-click on the field in which you want the text wrapped.

**3** Click on **Properties**.

**4** Go to the **Format tab** of the **Property Sheet** and set the **CanGrow property** to **Yes**, as shown.

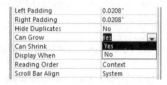

To modify a report's title, follow these steps.

**1** Open the report in the **Layout View**.

**2** On the **Format tab**, click on **Title** in the **Controls group**, as shown.

**3** A new label will appear in the report header. Change the text in the label as desired.

**4** Press **ENTER** when finished.

**Timesaver tip**

Need a tick box on your report? Drag the appropriate **Yes/No field** on to the report from the **Field List pane** and Access will create a tick box for you.

# → Modifying Your Report in the Design View

When you're in the Design View, you can see a fairly detailed representation of the structure of a report instead of the true layout of it. Figure 27.1 shows an example of a report in the Design View. You can't see the underlying data of the report while you're working in this view, which actually makes it easier to add controls, edit text boxes or change properties that are not available in the Layout View. In fact, some tasks, such as adding line numbers, can't even be performed in the Layout View.

Figure 27.1
A report open in the Design View.

To add line numbers to a report, follow these steps:

**1** Open the report in the **Design View**.

**2** Go to the **Design tab** and click on **Text Box** in the **Controls group**.

**3** Click on an open area of the report to place the text box. Remember to leave a little space to the left for the text box label.

**4** Click on the label and press **DELETE** on your keyboard.

**5** Select the text box and then click on it to position the cursor there.

**6** Type **1**. Press **ENTER**.

**7** On the data tab of the **Property Sheet**, set the **Running Sum property** to **Over All**. If the Property Sheet is not visible, press **F4**.

**8** Resize the text box as needed and then click on and drag it to a position on the left edge of the **Detail section**. When you switch to Layout, Report or Print View, you will see the line numbers.

## → Creating Alternating Row Colours

In Access 2007, report rows are all printed with the same background colour. Sometimes, however, it's helpful to have alternate rows in a different colour to improve readability.

To create alternating row colours in a report, follow these steps.

**1** Open the report in the **Design View**.

**2** If the Property Sheet is not visible, press **F4**.

**3** Click on the **Detail section header**.

**4** Click on the **Format tab** of the **Property Sheet**.

**5** Click on the **Alternate Back Color property box**.

**6** Select a colour theme. Click on the **ellipses button** to see the actual colours. Click on the **down arrow** to access colours by name.

**7** Click on the **Back Color property box** and select a colour theme for it, as shown, if desired. If you do not make a change here, the default colour is white.

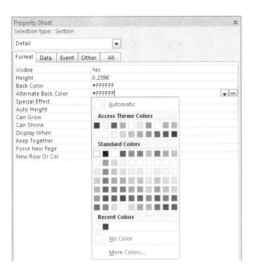

## 27

**8** Click on **Save** on the **Quick Access Toolbar**. The results will appear when you switch to the **Report View**, as shown in Figure 27.2.

| Product | Apr | May | Jun | Total |
|---|---|---|---|---|
| Northwind Traders Syrup | $500.00 | $0.00 | $0.00 | $500.00 |
| Northwind Traders Cajun Seasoning | $0.00 | $0.00 | $0.00 | $0.00 |
| Northwind Traders Olive Oil | $533.75 | $0.00 | $0.00 | $533.75 |
| Northwind Traders Boysenberry Spre | $0.00 | $0.00 | $0.00 | $0.00 |
| Northwind Traders Dried Pears | $0.00 | $0.00 | $0.00 | $0.00 |
| Northwind Traders Curry Sauce | $1,120.00 | $800.00 | $0.00 | $1,920.00 |
| Northwind Traders Fruit Cocktail | $0.00 | $0.00 | $0.00 | $0.00 |
| Northwind Traders Chocolate Biscuit | $230.00 | $0.00 | $0.00 | $230.00 |
| Northwind Traders Marmalade | $3,240.00 | $0.00 | $0.00 | $3,240.00 |
| Northwind Traders Scones | $200.00 | $0.00 | $0.00 | $200.00 |
| Northwind Traders Beer | $5,418.00 | $0.00 | $0.00 | $5,418.00 |
| Northwind Traders Crab Meat | $1,472.00 | $736.00 | $0.00 | $2,208.00 |
| Northwind Traders Clam Chowder | $772.00 | $0.00 | $0.00 | $772.00 |
| Northwind Traders Coffee | $0.00 | $0.00 | $0.00 | $0.00 |
| Northwind Traders Chocolate | $127.50 | $0.00 | $0.00 | $127.50 |
| Northwind Traders Dried Apples | $0.00 | $0.00 | $0.00 | $0.00 |
| Northwind Traders Long Grain Rice | $280.00 | $0.00 | $0.00 | $280.00 |
| Northwind Traders Ravioli | $1,950.00 | $0.00 | $0.00 | $1,950.00 |
| Northwind Traders Mozzarella | $3,132.00 | $0.00 | $0.00 | $3,132.00 |
| Northwind Traders Almonds | $0.00 | $200.00 | $0.00 | $200.00 |
| Northwind Traders Dried Plums | $0.00 | $52.50 | $0.00 | $52.50 |
| | $18,975.25 | $1,788.50 | $0.00 | $20,763.75 |

**Figure 27.2**

Alternating row colours can be used to highlight information and make it easier to read.

# 28

# Previewing, Printing and E-mailing a Report

In this lesson, you will learn how to view, print and e-mail a report.

## → Previewing Your Report

Before you print a report, it's a good idea to preview it. The Print Preview will show you exactly how the pages in the report will print. You can move through the report by using the navigation buttons at the bottom of the Access window.

To launch Print Preview, follow these steps.

**1** Go to the **Navigation pane** and right-click on the report you want to preview.

**2** Click on **Print Preview** in the shortcut menu, as shown.

When you are in Print Preview, right-click anywhere on the report. Another shortcut menu will launch, with a few previewing options for you. For example, you can select Zoom to resize the report so it is easier to view on your screen or Multiple Pages to see several pages of the report at once on the screen, as shown in Figure 28.1.

To close Print Preview, click on the Close Print Preview button in the Close Preview group on the Print Preview tab.

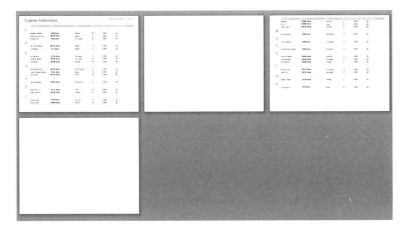

**Figure 28.1**
Previewing multiple pages before printing can help you to spot blank pages or other errors.

## Timesaver tip

If a report is open, right-click on its **document tab**, then click on **Print Preview** in the shortcut menu.

## → Printing Your Report

When you're ready to print your report, it shouldn't take long. Follow these steps to print all pages in a report when you don't need to use the Print dialogue box or commands from the Print tab.

**1** Right-click on the report you want to print in the **Navigation pane**.

**2** Click on **Print**.

**Timesaver tip**

The fastest way to print a report is to go to the Quick Access Toolbar and click on the Printer icon 🖶 . You can also use the **Print** command in the Microsoft Office button to locate the **Print**, **Quick Print**, and **Print Preview** commands.

If you only want to print specific pages of a report, follow these steps.

**1** Select the report in the **Navigation pane**. You do not need to open it.

**2** Click on the **Microsoft Office button**.

**3** Click on **Print**.

**4** In the **Print dialogue box**, set or modify the options as needed. For example, if you want to print specific pages, enter the page numbers in the **Pages From** section of **Print Range**, as shown.

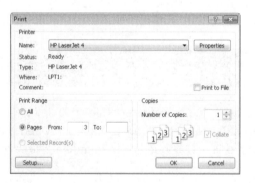

**5** Click on **Print**.

**Timesaver tip**

Click on **Setup** in the **Print dialogue box** to quickly change the setup for margins and columns.

# → E-mailing your Report

If you would prefer to e-mail the report to others rather than print it out, you can perform that task directly in Access 2007.

To send a report as an e-mail message, follow these steps.

**1** Click on the report you want to send in the **Navigation pane**.

**2** Click on the **Microsoft Office button**.

**3** Click on **E-mail**, as shown.

**4** Decide how you want to send the report (as an HTML, rich text, snapshot or text file). Make your selection in the **Send Object As dialogue box**.

**5** Click on **OK**.

**6** When the e-mail opens, it will have the report attached. Type in the recipients and a brief message. Click on **Send**.

28

## Jargon buster

**Rich text** is a text format that uses common formatting options, such as italics or font colours or layout, that are unavailable in a plain text format. When you choose this format to e-mail a report in, Access 2007 will apply HTML formatting codes to the report, which will make it look almost exactly as it does when opened in Access. Most people can easily open rich text and text files.

# 29

# Creating a Query

In this lesson, you will learn about queries, as well as how to create several different kinds of queries.

# → Understanding Queries

*Queries* are one of the areas where using a database has a clear advantage over a spreadsheet. With a query, you can obtain the answers to specific questions about your data without having to directly read the table data. Queries can filter data, perform calculations and summarise data quickly and easily. They can also automate a variety of data management tasks.

Essentially, a *query* is a request for data results or action on data or both. Well-designed databases use queries to assemble data from several different tables. Once a query has been created, you can run it to view the results by opening it in the Datasheet View. After that, it can be used as a record source for reports, forms or even other queries.

### Important

If your query will use two or more tables, they must be joined by a relationship. Read Chapter 10 for more details about relationships.

# → Creating a Select Query Using the Query Wizard

With a *select query*, you can create subsets of data to answer specific questions and then use that query to supply data to other database objects. A select query can access single or multiple tables.

To create a select query using the Query Wizard, follow these steps.

**1** Go to the **Create tab** and click on **Query Wizard** in the **Other group**.

**2** When the Wizard launches, click on **Simple Query Wizard**, as shown.

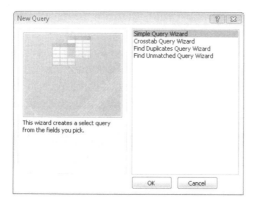

**3** Click on **OK**.

**4** Select the fields you want to use in your query. Place the available fields into **Selected Fields** by using the horizontal arrows.

**5** Click on **Next**.

**6** Decide whether you want a *detailed query* or a *summary query*. *Detailed queries* show every field of every record. Click on **Summary Options** if you choose a *summary query* and choose the summary values that you want it to calculate. Click on **OK**.

**7** Click on **Next**.

**8** Decide how you want to group the dates in your query. Click on **Next**.

**9** Type a title for the query and select **Open the query** to view the information.

**10** Click on **Finish**.

## Timesaver tip

If you discover that a query has been blocked by Access security measures, you will need to enable the blocked content. In the **Database Tools tab**, click on **Message Bar** in the **Show/Hide group**, if it is not already visible. On the **Message Bar**, click on **Options**. Click on **Enable This Content** and then click on **OK**.

# → Creating a Union Query

If you want to view all the records from two similar tables, you need to create a *union query* for the two tables. This process involves using SQL commands.

To create a union query, follow these steps.

**1** Go to the **Create tab** and click on **Query Design** in the **Other group**, as shown.

**2** In the **Show Table dialogue box**, click on **Close**.

**3** On the **Design tab**, click on **Union** in the **Query Type group**, as shown.

**4** At this point, the query will switch from the **Design View** to the **SQL View**. In the blank centre section of the query, you will enter it in SQL coding.

**5** Type **SELECT** in the **SQL View**. Enter the field names from the first table you want to query next to "SELECT", using square brackets – [ ] – to enclose each field name and a comma to separate the field names, as shown.

**6** Press **ENTER**. The cursor should move to the next line.

**7** Type **FROM** after the last name you typed in step 5 in the **SQL View**, then type the name of the first table you want to query, as shown.

SELECT [FIRST NAME],[LAST NAME]
FROM ORDERS

**8** Press **ENTER**. The cursor should move to the next line.

**9** To specify the criterion for a field from the first table, type **WHERE**. Type in the field name, a comparison operator and the criterion. This step is not required.

**10** Press **ENTER**. The cursor should move to the next line.

**11** Type **UNION** in the **SQL View**. Press **ENTER**. The cursor should move to the next line.

**12** Type **SELECT** in the **SQL View**. Enter the field names from the second table you want to query next to "SELECT", using square brackets as before to enclose each field name and a comma to separate the field names.

29

**13** Press **ENTER**. The cursor should move to the next line.

**14** Type **FROM** in the **SQL View**. Type the name of the second table you want to query.

**15** Press **ENTER**. The cursor should move to the next line.

**16** To specify criterion for a field from the second table, type **WHERE**. Type in the field name, a comparison operator and the criterion. This step is not required.

**17** Type a semicolon(;) to denote the end of the query.

**18** Go to the **Design tab** and click on **Run** in the **Results group**.

### Important

*Update queries* can set data in one or more fields to a null value, which has the same effect as deleting a portion of a record. However, an update query cannot add new records to a database or delete entire records from a database.

# → Creating and Running an Update Query

With an *update query*, you can change all data in a set of records. This type of query is used to add, change or delete data in one or more existing records. It can accept multiple criteria, which means that you can update a large number of records at once and change records in multiple tables at the same time.

To create an update query, follow these steps.

**1** Open the database containing the records that need updating.

**2** Go to the **Create tab** and click on **Query Design** in the **Other group**.

**3** In the **Show Table dialogue box**, select the table(s) with the records you need to update. Click on **Add**. Repeat this step until all the tables you need have been selected. The tables will appear as separate windows in the query designer.

**4** Click on **Close**.

**5** In each table window, double-click on the fields that you want updated. They will appear in the lower pane in the **Field row**.

**6** Enter the criteria as needed in the lower pane. An example criteria might be Not 'C' (this would find all records except the ones beginning with C).

**7** Go to the **Design tab** and click on **Run** in the **Results group**. Verify that the query is returning the proper records. Adjust the fields as needed. Return to the **Design View**.

**8** Go to the **Design tab** and click on **Update** in the **Query Type group**, as shown.

**9** Locate the field containing the data that you want changed. Type in a new expression (your change criteria) in the **Update to row** for the field.

**10** Go to the **Design tab** and click on **Run** in the **Results group**.

**11** When the alert message appears, click on **Yes**. The query will run and the data will be updated.

**Timesaver tip**

When adding fields in Query Designer, you can add all fields from a table instantly by double-clicking on the asterisk (*) at the top of the **Field list**.

## → Creating and Running an Append Query

**Important**

The results of an append query cannot be undone, so be certain that the information you are adding is accurate and complete.

An *append query* adds records from one or more source tables or queries to one or more destination tables. The source and destination tables do not need to reside in the same database.

To create and run an append query using the same database, follow these steps.

**1** Open the database containing the records you want to append.

**2** Go to the **Create tab** and click on **Query Design** in the **Other group**.

**3** In the **Show Table dialogue box**, select the tables and/or queries containing the records that you want to append. Click on **Add**.

**4** Click on **Close**.

**5** Double-click on the fields that you want to append. They will appear in the **Field row** in the lower pane.

**6** Enter the criteria as desired in the lower pane.

**7** Go to the **Design tab** and click on **Run** in the **Results group**. Verify that the results are what you expect.

**8** Right-click on the **document table** for the open query.

**9** Click on **Design View** in the shortcut menu.

**10** Go to the **Design tab** and click on **Append** in the **Query Type group**.

**11** In the **Append dialogue box**, decide whether to append records from one table to an existing table in the same database or have them go to an existing table in a different database. If you are copying records to a new table, you need to use a **make table query**, which is explained under "Creating a make table query" below.

**12** The query is now converted. In the **Append dialogue box**, click on **Current Database** and select the destination table using the **Table Name combo box**.

**13** Click on **OK**.

**14** Switch to the **Datasheet View** to preview your changes.

**15** Return to the **Design View** and click on **Run** in the **Results group**.

## Important

Don't leave a destination field blank – the query won't be able to append data to the field.

# → Creating a Make Table Query

When appending records to a new table, you need to create a make table query as part of the process. First, create a select query that returns the records you need for the new table. Then, follow these steps.

**1** Right-click on the **Query document tab**.

**2** Click on **Design View**.

**3** Go to the **Design tab** and click on **Make Table** in the **Query Type group**, as shown.

**4** In the **Make Table dialogue box**, type in a name for the new table using the **Table Name combo box**, as shown.

## 29

**5** To place the table in the open database, leave **Current Database** selected and click on **OK**. You're done. If you are placing the table in a *different* database, though, move to step 6.

**6** To place the table in another database, click on **Another Database**.

**7** Click on **Browse** to locate the other database.

**8** Click on **OK**.

**9** In the **Table Name combo box**, type in a new name for the table.

**10** Click on **OK**.

# 30

# Adding to a Query

In this lesson, you will learn how to add criteria and calculations to a query.

# → Adding Criteria to a Query

If you need to restrict the records returned in the results for a query, you will need to specify one or more criteria. *Query criteria* are basically conditions that are specified for a particular field. For example, 'Show only those records where the value of the city is Munich' is a valid criteria for a query. You might want to include additional criteria to further refine the results by adding an address, post code or phone field.

To add criteria to a query, follow these steps.

**1** Open a query in the **Design View**.

**2** In the **Criteria row** of a selected field, type in the new criteria. For example, you might enter 'Munich' in a 'City' field.

**3** In the **Criteria row** of a second selected field, type **Is Not Null AND<>""**. This criteria will be true whenever there is any known, non-empty value for a field. Repeat the step for a third or more fields.

**4** Switch to the **Datasheet View** to see the results of your query.

---

### Timesaver tip

To specify alternative criteria, you can use the **Criteria** and **Or rows** in the lower pane. If you need to specify more than two alternative criteria sets, use the rows below the **Or row**.

---

# → Adding Calculations to a Query

It is possible to calculate using information that is not stored within your tables. You can do that by creating a query that calculates and displays values based on the information you do have. For example, if you know the current date and a person's date of birth, you can create a query that continually updates the age of the person.

To add calculations to a query, follow these steps.

**1** Open a query in the **Design View**.

**2** Drag the field containing the information you do have on to the first blank column in the lower pane.

**3** In the second column, type an expression into the **Field row** that will calculate the data you need. For example, if you were calculating customer ages, you might type 'Age:DateDiff ("yyyy",[BirthDate], Date())' where 'Age' is the name of the calculated field.

**4** Switch to the **Datasheet View**. You should see the new fields there.

**30**

**Timesaver tip**

If you do not enter a name for the calculated field in your expression, Access will generate a generic name for it.

# 31

## Editing a Query

In this lesson, you will learn how to edit a query and find, hide or eliminate duplicate data.

# → Editing Data in a Query

Most of the time, you can edit the data in a query when you're in the Datasheet View. If a query is based on just one table or two tables that have a one-to-one relationship, you can always edit the data in a query, although you may discover that an occasional field cannot be edited.

Sometimes, however, Windows may just make a noise or nothing happens at all when you try to edit the data. If that occurs, you have tried to edit data that is:

■ SQL-specific

■ part of a cross-tab query

■ in a calculated field

■ is based on three or more tables and has a many-to-one-to-many relationship

■ contained in a query with a Group By clause.

In some cases, you can change the query so that it becomes an editable object. For example, you might decide to remove the calculations so that you can edit a field. Access 2007 Help and Support provides a list of ten different scenarios that can make a query datasheet available for editing (search for 'Edit Data in a Query' to see the list).

To manually edit records, follow these steps.

**1** Open a query in the **Datasheet View**.

**2** To delete content in a specific field, click on the field and enter a new value to edit a value in a specific field.

**3** To delete content in an entire row, select the row and press **DELETE** on the keyboard.

# → Finding, Hiding or Eliminating Duplicate Data

Duplicate data is usually not a problem in well-designed, newer databases. However, databases can often accumulate duplicate values over time as multiple people enter data. It's important to realise that sometimes a query can return records that seem to be duplicates, but they are, in fact, valid. This typically happens when fields in a query don't uniquely identify each record.

For the most part, duplications occur when:

■ two or more records contain duplicate fields, such as a double entry of a customer

■ two or more tables contain similar data, such as a Customers table and a Sales table that both contain records for the same customer

■ two or more databases contain similar data.

**31**

> ### Important
>
> When using the Find Duplicates Wizard, the query will only return matching records for values that match, character for character, in each field.

To find records with wholly or partially matched fields, follow these steps.

**1** In an open database, go to the **Create tab** and click on **Query Wizard** in the **Other group**.

**2** Click on **Find Duplicates Query Wizard**, as shown.

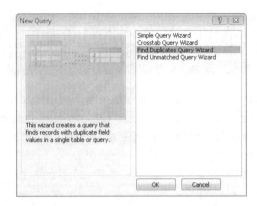

New Query

Simple Query Wizard
Crosstab Query Wizard
Find Duplicates Query Wizard
Find Unmatched Query Wizard

This wizard creates a query that
finds records with duplicate field
values in a single table or query.

OK    Cancel

**3** Click on **OK**. There may be an alert telling you that the feature has not been installed. Click on **Yes** and the Wizard will install.

**4** Select the table or query for the duplicate field search. Click on **Next**.

**5** Select the fields for the duplicate search using the horizontal arrows. Click on **Next**.

**6** Select any additional fields if prompted. Click on **Next**.

**7** Type in a name for the query.

**8** Select **View the Results**.

**9** Click on **Finish**.

### Timesaver tip

To customise the query to find partial matches, switch to the **SQL View** by right-clicking on the query's document tab and clicking on **SQL View**. Modify the SQL code as desired to locate and compare partial values.

To delete duplicate records, you will need to create and run a delete query. Follow these steps to create one.

**1** In an open database, go to the **Create tab** and click on **Query Design**.

**2** In the **Show Table dialogue box**, select the table on the 'one' side of the relationship. Click on **Add**.

**3** Click on **Close** in the **Show Table dialogue box**.

**4** Double-click on the asterisk in the table window to place all the fields in the lower pane.

**5** *Optional*: if you wish, add a column in the lower pane that allows you to enter criteria. Enter the criteria desired and clear the **Show** tick box for each criteria field. If you don't wish to add criteria, move to Step 6.

**6** Go to the **Design tab** and click on **Run** in the **Results group**.

**7** Go to the **Home tab** and click on the **Design View** in the **View group**.

**8** Go to the **Design tab** and click on **Delete** in the **Query Type group**.

**9** Verify that the **Delete row** in the *(all fields)* **column** displays **From** and that the **Criteria columns** display the word **Where**.

**10** Make one last check of the data as *you cannot undo the results once the query runs*.

**11** Click on **Run**.

**12** Click on **Yes** to delete the data.

---

**Important**

The results of a delete query cannot be undone, so be sure to back up your database before running one.

To remove duplicate records from your view without eliminating them, you must be using a query that includes two or more tables. Follow these steps.

**1** Open the query containing duplicate records in the **Design View**.

**2** Press **F4** to display the **Property Sheet**.

**3** In the **Property Sheet**, locate **Unique Records**, as shown. Set the property to **Yes**. This will allow the query to compare entire rows.

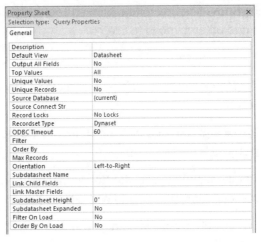

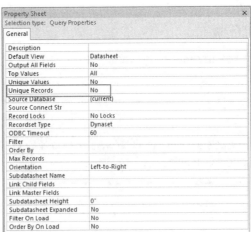

**4** Close the **Property Sheet**.

**5** Switch to the **Datasheet View**.

---

**Important**

When the **Unique Records property** is set to **Yes**, it might seem as if you are still seeing duplicate records. This can happen when similar information is in two tables (for example an order might be received and sent on the same date, so the records will both show the same date), but they aren't truly duplicate. In such cases, consider changing the **Unique Values property** to **Yes** so that your query doesn't look at the underlying tables for duplicates. Instead, it will look at the values of the fields and, if two fields match for two records, it will hide one record from your view.

---

If you want to show hidden field, follow these steps:

**1** Open the query in the **Datasheet View**.

**2** Right-click on the **header row**.

**3** Click on **Unhide Columns**.

**4** Select each field you want added to the datasheet.

**5** Click on **OK**.

31

# 32

# Summarising and Saving Queries

In this lesson, you will learn how to summarise
query values and save query results.

# → Summarising Query Values

When you want to summarise information in a query, you will need to create a parameter query. This type of query lets you design a query that prompts you to supply pieces of information, which are the parameters (limits) for the query. For each parameter, the query will display a separate dialogue box asking you for the value involved.

## Important

Parameter queries can be created from Select, Crosstab, Append, Make Table and Update queries.

To create a parameter query, follow these steps.

**1** Create or open a select query in the **Design View**.

**2** For every row where you want a parameter applied, type in the text for the parameter in the **Criteria row** of the lower pane. The text should be enclosed by brackets. For example, [Country/city]. Repeat this step for each parameter needed.

**3** On the **Design tab**, click on **Run** in the **Results group**.

**4** The **Parameter dialogue box** prompt will appear, as shown. Type in the parameter.

**5** Click on **OK**.

## → Saving Query Results

You need to create and run a make table query when you want to save the results of a select query as a new table. This process tells Access to actually create a new table in the current database using the information from other tables in the same database.

> **Important**
>
> Even though you can save a select query, only the design of a query is saved, not the results. Because tables and underlying information can change each time the query runs, the results will often differ. That's why a make table query must be created – it holds the results as a separate table.

To save the results of a select query, follow these steps.

**1** In the **Design View**, open and run the select query involved.

**2** If a security warning appears in the message bar, as shown, click on **Options**, then on **Enable This Content**.

Security Warning   Certain content in the database has been disabled   Options...

**3** Go to the **Home tab** and click on **Design View** in the **Views group**.

**4** Go to the **Design tab** and click on **Make Table** in the **Query Type group**.

**5** In the **Make Table dialogue box**, type in the name of the new table and decide whether you want the table placed in the current database or in a different one. Click on **OK**.

**6** In the **Design tab**, click on **Run** in the **Results group**.

32

**7** If a deletion warning appears, click on **OK**.

**8** Click on **Yes** in the **Confirmation dialogue box**. The rows will be pasted into a new table.

## Timesaver tip

If you want to collect a parameter but have the query return rows for which other comparisons evaluate as true, type in a comparison operator to the left of the first square bracket that is enclosing the parameter prompt. For example, prompt for a date and return dates where the value of the year is greater than the parameter by typing >[Date].

# 33

# Joining Tables and Queries

In this lesson, you will learn how to use inner and outer joins in your queries, as well as unequal joins. You will also discover how to compare two tables using joins and remove a join.

When relationships are used to connect tables, they connect at the fields that they have in common. This connection is represented in the relationship as a *join*.

## → Using Inner Joins

*Inner joins* are used when you want to return only the rows from both tables in the join that match on a joining field. Access 2007 automatically creates inner joins when related tables are added in the Design View. It also adds inner joins when you add two tables to a query where the tables both have fields with the same or compatible data types and one of the join fields is a primary key.

To create an inner join, follow these steps.

**1** Right-click on the query in the **Navigation pane** and click on the **Design View**.

**2** Click on and drag a field from one data source to a field on another data source.

**3** A new line will form between the two tables, showing the join.

## → Using Outer Joins

An *outer join* is used when you want all rows from one table in the join to be included in the results *and* you want the query to return only those rows from the other table that match the first table in the joining field. An outer join is created by modifying inner joins.

To create an outer join, follow these steps.

**1** In a query's **Design View**, double-click on the join that will change, as shown.

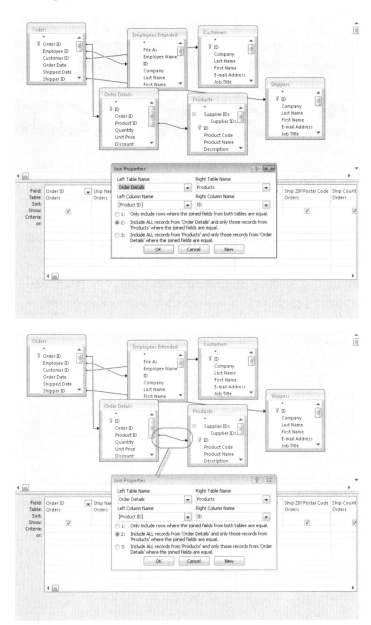

**2** In the **Join Properties dialogue box**, choose a selection from the numbered options. In the illustration, number three would be selected to create the outer join.

**3** Click on **OK**.

**4** When the new join displays, an arrow will point from the all rows data source to the matching rows data source.

## → Using Cross Joins

*Cross joins* are not plainly represented in Access 2007, as inner and outer joins are. A cross join takes each row from a table and combines it with each row from another table to make a cross product (also known as a Cartesian product). When you run a query where the tables are not clearly joined, a cross join is the result.

Cross joins are typically used when you want to examine every potential combination of rows between tables or queries. For example, if you want to give a bonus to every sales employee based on certain products sold, you would build a query that sums up each employee's sales for individual products, create a table that has potential bonus percentages and then combine the two in a query that performs a cross join. The final results would show hypothetical bonuses for each employee.

---

### Important

Cross joins can produce huge numbers of rows in query results and may take a very long time to run.

---

# → Using Unequal Joins

Not every join is based on the equivalence of the joined fields. Joins not based on equivalences are known as *unequal joins*. They are used when you need to combine the rows of two data sources based on field values that aren't equal.

Unequal joins are almost always based on the following comparison operators:

■ greater than (>)

■ less than (<)

■ greater than or equal to (>=)

■ less than or equal to (<=).

If you want to use an unequal join, follow these basic steps.

**1**   Create a join in the **Design View**.

**2**   Switch to the **SQL View** by clicking on **View** in the **Results group** on the **Design tab**. Click or **SQL View**, as shown.

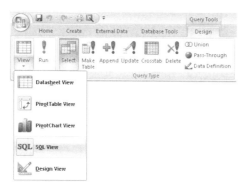

**3**   Find the equals (=) comparison operator and change it to one of the operators listed above.

**4**   Click on **Run** in the **Results group** under the **Design tab**.

**Important**

When you have created an unequal join in the SQL view, you cannot open the query again in the Design view until you have changed the comparison operator back to equals (=) in the SQL View.

## → Removing a Join

If you accidentally create a join, you can remove it by following these steps.

**1** Right-click on the query in the **Navigation pane** and click on the **Design View**.

**2** In the lower pane, click on the join that you want to remove.

**3** Press **DELETE** on the keyboard.

**Timesaver tip**

To determine which table is the left or right table in a join, double-click on the join and check the **Join Properties dialogue box**. If you prefer, switch to the **SQL View** and examine the **FROM clause**.

# 34

# Using Multivalued Fields in a Query

In this lesson, you will learn how to display a multivalued field in a query, insert a single value into a multivalued field and search for more than one value in a multivalued field. In addition, you'll discover how to display a bound value in a query and use a query as a mail merge data source.

Multivalued fields allow you to select and store more than one choice in a field without creating an advanced database. For example, if you have a task that must be assigned to multiple people, a multivalued field allows you to store each person's name in the same field for the task. Each name is separated by a comma.

## Important

Access 2007 can provide multivalued fields because it doesn't actually store the values in a single field, even though that's what you see on the screen.

# → Displaying a Multivalued Field in a Query

Before you complete the following steps, decide whether you want the multivalued field to display values separated by commas or as separate rows.

## Important

Multivalued fields are new in Access 2007. They are lookup fields designed to replace the display of a number such as an ID with something more meaningful – a name or address, for example, so Access can display an employee's name instead of his or her ID number. The employee's ID number is the bound value and the employee's name is the display value.

Follow these steps.

**1** Click on the **Microsoft Office button**.

**2** Click on **Open**.

**3** Select and open the database.

**4** Go to the **Create tab** and click on **Query Design** in the **Other group**.

**5** Click on the table containing the multivalued field in the **Show Table box**.

**6** Click on **Add**.

**7** Click on **Close**.

**8** Click on and drag the field that you want to use into the lower pane.

**9** Go to the **Design tab** and click on **Run** in the **Results group**.

---

**Timesaver tip**

To display the individual values in a multivalued field, change the **Value property** by appending the string '**.Value**' to '**AssignedTo**' in the **Field row** of the lower pane.

---

## → Searching for More Than One Value in a Multivalued Field

To search for more than one value in a multivalued field, you will need to specify several criteria for that field. To do that, follow these steps.

**1** Click on the **Microsoft Office button**.

**2** Click on **Open**.

**3** Select and open the database.

**4** Go to the **Create tab** and click on **Query Design** in the **Other group**.

**5** Click on the table containing the multivalued field in the **Show Table box**.

**6** Click on **Add.**

**7** Click on **Close**.

34

**8** Click on and drag the field that you want to use into the lower pane.

**9** Under **AssignedTo**, type in the bound value for each field in each **Criteria row**, as shown.

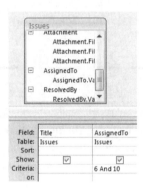

**10** Go to the **Design tab** and click on **Run** in the **Results group**.

# → Displaying a Bound Value in a Query

By default, the display value for a bound value is automatically shown in the Datasheet View. You will need to override this default to display the bound value in a query. To do that, follow these steps.

**1** Click on the **Microsoft Office button**.

**2** Click on **Open**.

**3** Select and open the database.

**4** Go to the **Create tab** and click on **Query Design** in the **Other group**.

**5** Click on the table containing the multivalued field in the **Show Table box**.

**6** Click on **Add**.

**7** Click on **Close**.

**8** Click on and drag the field that you want to use into the lower pane.

**9** Click on the **AssignedTo.Value field**.

**10** Go to the **Design tab** and click on **Property Sheet** in the **Show/Hide group**.

**11** Click on the **Lookup tab** in the **Property Sheet**. Select **Text Box** in the **Display Control property**.

## → Using a Query as a Mail Merge Source

Queries are a great source for letters, e-mail messages, labels, envelopes and directories. While this process is typically done using Word 2007, to use an Access query as a mail merge source for a Word 2007 letter, follow these steps.

**1** Open the database you want to use as the source for the mail merge.

**2** In the **Navigation pane**, click on the query that you want to use.

**3** Go to the **External Data tab** and click on **More** in the **Export group**.

**4** Click on **Merge it with Microsoft Office Word**, as shown in illustration on page 232.

**5** In the **Microsoft Word Mail Merge Wizard**, select whether you want the link created in an existing document or a new one. Click on **OK**. **Note:** If you are linking to an existing document, you will need to locate and select the file in the **Select Microsoft Word Document dialogue box**. Click on **Open**.

**34**

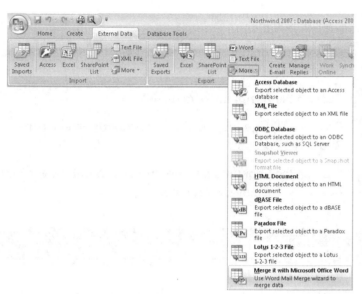

**6** It might take a few seconds for the Word document to open. When it does, go to the **Mail Merge pane** on the right side of the Word document and click on **Letters** under **Select document type**, as shown.

**7** Click on **Next: Starting Document**.

**8** Click on **Next: Select Recipients**.

**9** Verify that **Use an existing list** has been selected and the correct name for the query has been displayed under **Use an existing list**, as shown on next page. Click on **Edit recipient list** if you need to customise the contents of the query and then click on **OK**. Otherwise, move to step 10.

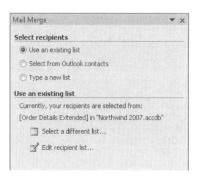

**10** Click on **Next: Write Your Letter**. Type or paste your content into the Word document.

**11** Click on **Next: Preview Your Letters**. Preview merged letters using the horizontal arrows as needed and make changes to the recipient list if necessary.

**12** Click on **Next: Complete the Merge**.

**13** Under **Merge**, select whether you want to merge directly to print or want to edit individual letters.

**14** In the **Print dialogue box**, make the selections you desire. Click on **OK**.

**34**

**Timesaver tip**

You can use a table as a mail merge source, too. Follow the steps for using a query as the source, but just use a table instead. Also, you may have noticed in the Mail Merge pane that additional options besides Letters are available. If you prefer one of those options, simply click on the one you want and follow the prompts.

# 35

# Working with Attachments

In this lesson, you will learn how to work with attachments in Access 2007. Specifically, you will learn how to add an attachment field to a table as well as how to attach a field to a table, use attachments with forms and reports or save attached files to other locations. You will also learn how to remove attached files.

## → Adding an Attachment Field to a Table

Attachment data types are new in Access 2007. Just as you attach files to e-mail messages, you can attach files to the records in your database. All you need to do is make sure that you have an attachment field in your table. This new process lets you open documents in their original programs (as long as you have that program installed) and compresses the attachment as needed so that your database doesn't get out of control.

### Important

After you set the data type to Attachment for a field, you cannot change it. A maximum of two gigabytes of data can be attached, with individual files not exceeding 256 megabytes in size. If you can't seem to attach a file, check the maximums mentioned here. You may have exceeded Access 2007's limits.

To add an attachment field to a table, follow these steps.

**1** Open the desired table in the **Datasheet View**. Click on the first available blank new field.

**2** Go to the **Datasheet tab** and click on the down arrow for **Data Type** in the **Data Type & Formatting group**. Click on **Attachment**, as shown.

**3** The field will be set to the Attachment data type and a paperclip icon will be placed in the header row of the field, as shown.

**4** Click on **Save** in the **Quick Access Toolbar**.

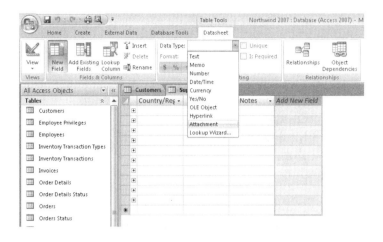

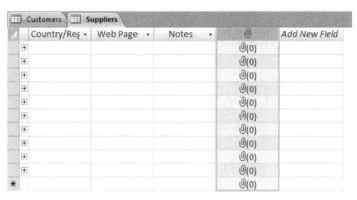

### Timesaver tip

You can open an attached file when a table is open in the **Datasheet View**. Just double-click on the attachment cell and then double-click on the file you want to see in the **Attachments dialogue box**.

35

## → Attaching a Field Directly to a Table

Once you have added an attachment field to a table, files can be directly attached to it.

**1** In a table that has an attachment field, double-click on the attachment field record.

**2** In the **Attachments dialogue box**, click on **Add**, as shown.

**3** Locate and click on the attachment in the **Choose File window**. Click on **Open**. Repeat steps 2 and 3 to add more attachments.

**4** Click on **OK** in the **Attachments dialogue box**. A number will appear in the **Attachment field** indicating the number of attachments for that record, as shown.

**Important**

To view an attachment directly from a table, you need to have the proper program for that file installed. If you don't, a dialogue box will appear asking you to select another program to use to view the file.

# → Using Attachments with Forms and Reports

There will be occasions when you want to use an attachment with a form or report. In those cases, you need to use the *attachment control*. It automatically makes image files as you navigate through records in a database. So, for example, if you attach a Word document to a file, Access 2007 will display a corresponding file type icon.

To add the attachment control to a form or a report, follow these steps.

**1** Right-click on the form or report in the **Navigation pane**.

**2** Click on the **Design View** in the shortcut menu.

**3** Go to the **Design tab** and click on **Add Existing Fields** in the **Tools group**, as shown. This should launch the **Field List pane**.

**Timesaver tip**

Launch the **Field List pane** quickly by pressing **Alt + F8**.

**4** Locate the attachments in the **Field List pane**. You might need to expand several items if you don't remember where the attachment is located. Click on and drag the *entire* attachment field from the list on to the form, as shown. Include all items. Drop it where you want it to go in the form.

**5** If you want to modify the property for the control that was created in step 4, right-click on the control and then click on **Properties**. Modify the control properties as desired.

**6** Click on **Save** in the **Quick Access Toolbar**.

**7** Right-click on the **Document tab** and then click on **Form View** or **Report View**, as applicable. This action opens the form or report for viewing.

## → Saving Attached Files to Other Locations

If you need to save an attached file to another location on your hard drive or network, it's an easy process. Just follow these steps.

**1** Open the object containing the attachments.

**2** Double-click on the **attachment record**.

**3** In the **Attachments dialogue box**:

■ click on **Save As** to save a single file, navigate to the location where you want to save the file and click on **Save**

■ click on **Save All** to save all files in the object, navigate to the location where you want to save the file and click on **Select**.

**4** Click on **OK** in the **Attachments dialogue box**.

**Important**

When you select **Save All**, you can't pick and choose the files that you save – you *must* save them all. If you need to selectively save files, use the **Save As** option and repeat the saving process for each file.

## → Removing Attached Files

When you want to remove an attached file from a record, follow these steps.

**1** Double-click on the **attachment field** in the table.

**2** In the **Attachments dialogue box**, select the file that you want to remove. Click on **Remove**.

**35**

# 36

# Importing and Exporting

In this lesson, you will learn about basic importing and exporting operations. You'll discover how to run, save and schedule an import or export operation as a specification and create an Outlook task to run that operation.

## → Understanding Importing and Exporting Operations

Importing and exporting content is common in Access 2007. Sometimes you need data from another source besides Access; sometimes you will need to place content from a database into another source. The import and export operations involve saving the settings used with the Import or Export Wizard so that the next time you need to perform the same task, Access can repeat the process without your input.

To make it even easier for you, Access 2007 has been integrated with Outlook 2007 so you can schedule or run an import/export operation directly from Outlook.

## → Running, Saving and Scheduling an Import Operation as a Specification

Every time you run the Import or Export Wizard in Access, the settings used can be saved as a *specification*. This specification is what allows you to repeat the operation in the future without providing any input.

Even though you don't have to add anything when you run a specification, you can make changes to it when you need to. Maybe you want to change the source file, for example – you can easily do that before the specification runs.

For the following instructions, it is assumed that you are importing information from Excel 2007.

## Important

You can only import one worksheet at a time when importing from Excel 2007. If you want to import multiple worksheets, you will need to repeat the importing process for each worksheet. Also, note that a maximum of 255 source columns can be imported.

When you need to create an import specification, follow these steps.

**1** In **Excel**, locate the source file and select the worksheet that you want to import into Access. You can define a named range in Excel if you want only a portion of the worksheet to be imported.

**2** Close the source workbook. If you keep it open, it can cause errors during the import operation.

**3** Open the Access database where you want the imported information to go. Note that:

■ you must have permission to make changes to the database and it *cannot* be opened as read-only

■ you need to decide whether the data will be stored in a new or existing table – create a new table if necessary.

**4** Go to the **External Data tab** and click on **Excel** in the **Import group**, as shown.

36

**5** In the **Get External Data – Excel Spreadsheet dialogue box**, determine the source of the data and how and where the data should be stored in Access (as shown), as follows:

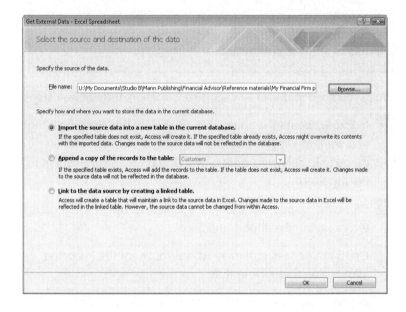

- select **Import the source data into a new table in the current database** if you want to store data in a new table

- select **Append a copy of the records to the table** if you want to append the data to an existing table – use the dropdown list to select the existing table

- select **Link to the data source by creating a linked table** if you just want a link to the Excel file.

**6** Click on **OK**. The **Import Spreadsheet Wizard** will launch, as shown.

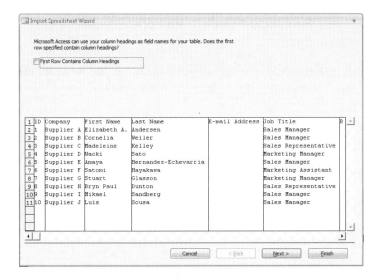

**7** In the **Import Spreadsheet Wizard**, you will be prompted for additional information from Access depending on the choice you made in step 5. Make selections as the prompts indicate, clicking on **Next** to move through the prompts and then on **Finish** to complete the process. Here are some tips to help you complete the Wizard.

■ Access will use Excel column headings to name fields in a new table, but you can change the names either during or after the import operation. If you are appending data, however, all column headings in Excel and Access must match.

■ When reviewing field properties, click on a column in the lower half of the page to see the corresponding field properties. Access will analyse the first eight rows in every column to suggest a data type, but you should review and edit the name and data type for each field as desired. Keep in mind that values not compatible with the data type you choose will either be ignored or converted incorrectly.

■ If you decide to let Access add the primary key, an **AutoNumber field** will be added to your destination table and populated with ID values beginning with the number 1.

36

**8** Select **Save Import steps** to save operation details for future use.

**9** Type a name for the import specification in the **Save as text box**, as shown. Add a description if you like.

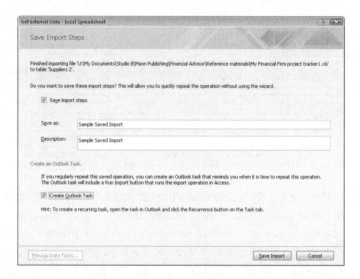

**10** To perform the operation at specific intervals, select **Create Outlook Task**.

**11** Click on **Save Import**. An **Outlook task dialogue box** will launch, as shown.

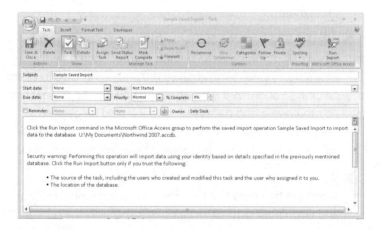

**12** Review and edit the task settings (due date, reminder and so on) in **Outlook**.

**13** Click on **Save & Close**.

## Timesaver tip

Import/export operations can be done in any file format that Access supports. However, the details of a linking operation or an operation where only a portion of the datasheet is exported cannot be saved.

If you are importing from other sources, follow these basic steps.

**1** Go to the **External Data tab** and click on **More** in the **Import group**.

**2** Click on the **source type** from the menu, as shown.

**3** Follow the Wizard's instructions to complete the import.

36

## Timesaver tip

Export specifications that send formatted data to Excel or Word 2007 will use the current filter and column settings in Access. For the most accurate export, be sure to close the source object in Access. Otherwise, the export operation will only send the data that is displayed in the current view of the source object.

## → Running, Saving and Scheduling an Export Operation as a Specification

The Access export operation is very similar to its import operation. Follow these steps to export data into Excel files.

**1** In an open database, go to the **External Data tab** and click on **Excel** in the **Export group**, as shown.

**2** Locate and select the destination file and format. When specifying export options, keep the following in mind.

■ Select **Export data with formatting and layout** if you want to preserve your database details in Excel.

■ Select **Open the destination file after the export operation is complete** if you want to view the results of the export operation. You can only choose this option when exporting formatted data.

■ Select **Export only the selected records** if you want to export formatted data and specific records.

**3** Click on **OK**.

**4** Select **Save Export steps** to save operation details for future use.

**5** Type a name for the export specification in the **Save as text box**. Add a description if you like.

**6** To perform the operation at specific intervals, select **Create Outlook Task**.

**7** Click on **Save Export**. An **Outlook task dialogue box** will launch.

**8** Review and edit the task settings (due date, reminder and so on) in **Outlook**.

**9** Click on **Save & Close**.

36

# 37

# Printing in Access

In Chapter 28, you learned about printing *reports*. In this lesson, you will learn how to print *other* objects in Access, as well as how to create and print *labels*.

# → Printing an Access File

Because it's easier to arrange a database into sections using a report format, Access files are usually printed as reports. However, there may be occasions when you want to print a table or another object. To do that, follow these steps.

**1** Select the object from the **Navigation pane**.

**2** Go to the **Microsoft Office button** and hover the cursor over **Print**, as shown.

**3** Three print options will appear.

■ Select **Print** if you need to specify printing options, such as a certain printer, the number of copies or other options, as shown. Click on **OK** to finalise the print.

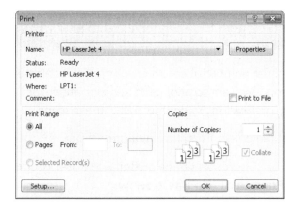

■ Select **Quick Print** if you don't have any changes or specifications you want to make. The object will be sent instantly to your printer.

■ Select **Print Preview** if you want to see how the pages will appear when printed, as shown. This option lets you make a variety of changes using the **Print Preview** tab before printing. When you have completed your changes, click on **Close Print Preview**. Go back to the **Microsoft Office button** and click on **Print**.

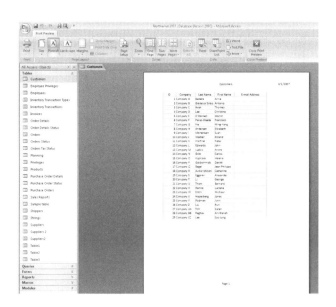

37

## → Printing in Landscape Orientation

Because of the number of columns in a typical database object, you will probably want to print most items in *landscape* (horizontal) orientation. To do that, follow these steps.

**1** Select the object from the **Navigation pane**.

**2** Go to the **Microsoft Office button** and hover your cursor over **Print**. Click on **Print Preview**.

**3** Click on **Landscape** in the **Page Layout group** of the **Print Preview tab**. The document will then display in landscape view.

**4** Go to the **Microsoft Office button** and click on **Print**.

**5** In the **Print dialogue box**, click on **Properties**.

**6** In the **Layout tab**, verify that **Landscape** has been selected under **Orientation**, as shown.

**7** Click on **OK**.

**8** In the **Print dialogue box**, click on **OK**.

# → Creating and Printing Labels

You can use Access to print labels, too. When you do, the labels are actually created as a report, formatted to a small page size that fits the label. When you print labels, Access retrieves the information from the tables or queries containing the information. Each address is a single label in the Access report.

To print labels, follow these steps.

**1** Select the table or query record source in the **Navigation pane**.

**2** Go to the **Create tab** and click on **Labels** in the **Reports group**, as shown.

**3** In the **Label Wizard**, select the label size from the list provided, as shown, or click on **Customize** to create your own.

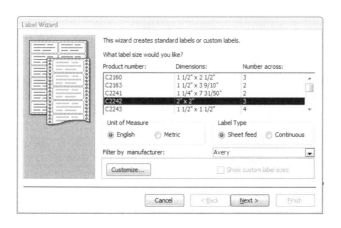

**4** Click on **Next**.

**5** Choose the font, size, weight and colour you want to use. Click on **Next**.

**6** Choose the fields for your label by selecting a field and using the horizontal arrow to place the field on the prototype label. Then you can do the following.

- You can add a space between fields by using your cursor and pressing the **space bar** on your keyboard.

- Create a new line in the prototype label by pressing **ENTER** on the keyboard.

- Remove a field by pressing **backspace** on the keyboard.

- Add text by placing the cursor where you want to add the text. Type in the information.

**7** Click on **Next**. Choose any fields that are necessary if you want to sort the labels.

**8** Click on **Next**.

**9** Type in a name for the report and select **See the labels as they will look printed** or **Modify the label design** if you want the report displayed in the **Design View** so that you can make any final changes, as shown.

**10** Click on **Finish**.

---

### Timesaver tip

If your data is not lining up correctly, make changes in the **Design View** or in **Print Preview** using the **Page Setup dialogue box**. You can change grid settings, column sizes and column layouts using this method.

---

```
Company A          Company AA              Company B
Bedecs Anna        Toh Karen               Gratacos Solsona
Owner              Purchasing Manager      Antonio
                                           Owner




Company BB         Company C               Company CC
Raghav Amritansh   Axen Thomas             Lee Soo Jung
Purchasing Manager Purchasing              Purchasing Manager
                   Representative




Company D          Company E               Company F
Lee Christina      O'Donnell Martin        Pérez-Olaeta Francisco
Purchasing Manager Owner                   Purchasing Manager
```

H  ◄ 1        ► ►I ►  ⅍ No Filter

## → Customising Labels

To print customised labels, follow these steps.

**1** Select the table or query record source in the **Navigation pane**.

**2** Go to the **Create tab** and click on **Labels** in the **Reports group**.

**3** In the **Label Wizard**, click on **Customize**, as shown.

**37**

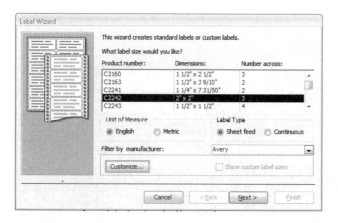

**4** In the **New Label Size dialogue box**, click on **New**. The
**New Label dialogue box** will launch, as shown.

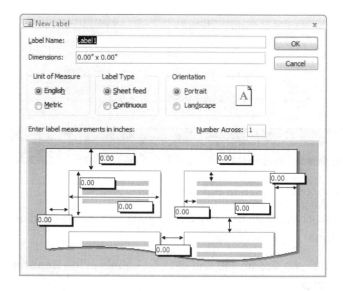

**5** Enter your custom measurements and details into the
**Dimensions** and **Unit of Measure** sections. The default will
be 0.00. Enter your figures by placing the cursor directly in
the measurement box, as shown, *not* in the Dimensions
section above.

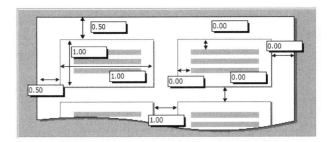

**6** Select **Sheet Feed** or **Continuous** under **Label Type**, then select **Portrait** or **Landscape** under **Orientation**. Click on **OK**.

**7** Click on **Close**.

**8** In the **Label Wizard**, verify that your customised label has been selected. Click on **Next**.

**9** Choose the font, size, weight and colour you want to use. Click on **Next**.

**10** Choose the fields for your label by selecting a field and using the horizontal arrow to place the field on the prototype label. Then you can do the following.

■ You can add a space between fields by using your cursor and pressing the **space bar** on your keyboard.

■ Create a new line in the prototype label by pressing **ENTER** on the keyboard.

■ Remove a field by pressing **backspace** on the keyboard.

■ Add text by placing the cursor where you want to add the text. Type in the information.

**11** Click on **Next**. Choose any fields that are necessary if you want to sort the labels.

**12** Click on **Next**.

37

**13** Type in a name for the report and select **See the labels as they will look printed** or **Modify the label design** if you want the report displayed in the **Design View** so that you can make any final changes.

**14** Click on **Finish**.

## Timesaver tip

Want to print addresses directly on to envelopes instead of labels? Click on **Customize** in step 1 of the Wizard and then follow the instructions in step 4 to specify the envelope settings. Don't forget to set the label type to **Sheet Feed**.

# 38

## Using Macros

In this lesson, you will learn the basics of using macros in Access 2007, including how to create, run, fix and enable or disable a macro.

# → Understanding Macros

A *macro* is a great tool to use because it makes a lot of things run more easily and smoothly in a relational database than they would otherwise. Macros perform a specific series of actions and can be embedded into the event properties of forms, reports and controls. This saves you time you because tasks that you perform often become automated, so you don't have to remember to do them – they are simply performed as needed.

Macros are essentially simple pieces of programming that build lists of actions to perform. Don't let the word 'programming' scare you, however – macros are really very simple to write and use.

A macro consists of individual macro *actions*, each of which requires one or more arguments. You can assign a name to every macro in a macro group and add conditions to specify how each macro action should run. Actions are critical to a macro – without them, macros don't exist. Some examples of macro actions are finding a record or applying a filter to a report.

**Jargon buster**

When you **embed** a macro, it means that you are making the macro an actual part of the object or control involved. Embedded macros make databases easier to manage because the macro is always there whether you copy, import or export a form or report.

# → New Macro Features in Access 2007

Macros have always been a big part of Access but, with Access 2007, there are some new features to be aware of that help to reduce the need to write code. The new features are as follows.

■ **Embedded macros** — You can embed a macro into any event provided by a form, report or control.

■ **Increased security** — When reviewing a database, Access will stop some macros from running unless you specifically enable trusted status for the database.

■ **Error handling and debugging** — Three new macro actions can help you to identify and perform specific actions when errors occur as your macro is running. The new actions are OnError, ClearMacroError and SingleStep.

■ **Temporary variables** — Another three macro actions let you create and use temporary variables in your macros. These are SetTempVar, RemoveTempVar and RemoveAllTempVars.

**Jargon buster**

Most macros are standalone objects, but they can be combined into **macro groups** – a single macro object that contains multiple macros.

## → Creating a Macro

There are several ways in which you can create a macro. This section will focus on *standalone macros* and *macro groups*. To create and run a *standalone macro*, follow these steps.

**1** Go to the **Create tab** and click on **Macro** in the **Other group**, as shown.

38

**2** When the **Macro Builder** opens, click on the first empty cell in the **Action column**.

**3** Use the down arrow to display a list of macro actions, as shown. Select the action that you want.

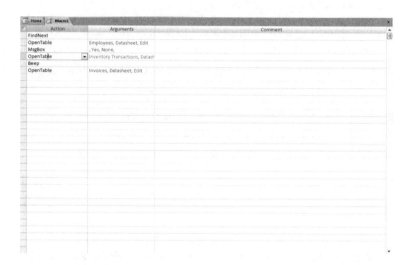

**4** Arguments are automatically entered when you select an action that requires one. You can modify arguments using the **Action Arguments pane**, as shown, so do that now if necessary.

**5** Type in a comment in the **Comment column** if desired.

**6** Right-click on the **Macro document tab**. Click on **Save**.

**7** Name the macro. Click on **OK**.

**8** In the **Design tab**, click on **Run** in the **Tools group**.

**9** Click on **OK** if a caution dialogue box appears. All the objects containing the macro you have just created will open. If any macros have errors, an error message will appear to help you resolve them, as shown.

To create and run a *macro group*, follow these steps.

**1** Open a macro in the **Design View**.

**2** Go to the **Design tab** and click on **Macro Names** in the **Show/Hide group**, as shown.

**3** The macro should now show a column called **Macro Name** to the left of the **Action column**. In this column, type a name for the first macro in the group.

**38**

**4** In the **Action column**, add the actions you want the first macro to perform, as shown.

**5** In the **Action Arguments pane**, add any arguments required.

### Timesaver tip

Actions can also be created by dragging a database object directly from the Navigation Pane into an empty row in the Macro Builder.

**6** Move to the next empty row and repeat steps 3 to 5 for each macro in the group.

**7** Right-click on the **Macro document tab** and then click on **Save**.

**8** Name the macro. Click on **OK**.

**9** In the **Design tab**, click on **Run** in the **Tools group**.

### Timesaver tip

If you have an argument that has a setting of a database object name, drag the object from the **Navigation pane** to the action's **Object Name argument box**. The argument will be instantly set.

# → Fixing a Macro

When you need to fix a macro, you can watch the macro's flow and resulting actions by stepping through the macro step by step. To do that, follow these steps.

**1** In the **Navigation pane**, right-click on the macro. Click on **Design View** in the shortcut menu.

**2** Go to the **Design tab** and click on **Single Step** in the **Tools group**, as shown.

**3** In the same **Tools group**, click on **Run**.

**4** The **Macro Single Step dialogue box** will launch, as shown.

**5** If there is a '0' in the **Error Number box**, the macro has no errors. Otherwise, a different error number will appear.

**6** To carry out the action shown in the dialogue box, click on **Step**. Repeat this step, reviewing each action and checking for errors. When all errors have been stepped through, the **Macro Single Step dialogue box** will close.

**38**

## Timesaver tip

You can close the **Macro Single Step dialogue box** by clicking on **Stop All Macros** or, if you prefer to turn off the single step process, you can click on **Continue** to run the remainder of the macro.

## → Enabling or Disabling Macros

Before any macro can run in Access, the Trust Center (explained in more detail in Chapter 39) will perform several checks. If any potential problem is detected, the macro will be disabled and a Security Warning will appear in the message bar below the Ribbon, as shown.

### Timesaver tip

You can enable *all* content by using the **Trust Center** in **Access Options**. However, this is a potentially dangerous setting to use, especially if you routinely receive content from unknown publishers. It's highly recommended never to use this setting.

To *enable* the content in a specific macro that has been blocked, follow these steps.

**1** Click on **Options** in the **Message Bar**.

**2** Select **Enable this content** in the **Security Alert dialogue box**, as shown.

**3** Click on **OK**.

If you need to *disable* a macro, follow these steps.

**1** Click on the **Microsoft Office button** and click on **Access Options**.

**2** Click on **Trust Center**.

**3** Click on **Trust Center Settings** under **Microsoft Office Access Trust Center**.

**4** Click on **Macro Settings** in the left pane.

**5** Determine the disabling option you want from the following.

- Select **Disable all macros without notification** if you don't trust macros and want them *all* disabled.

- Select **Disable all macros with notification** if you do want macros disabled, but want to receive security alerts. This is the default setting in Access 2007.

- Select **Disable all macros except digitally signed macros** if you are willing to accept those from trusted publishers.

**6** Click on **OK**.

### Timesaver tip

Need to run a macro fast? Right-click on it in the **Navigation pane**, then click on **Run** in the shortcut menu. One other tip: you can single step through a macro as it is running by pressing **CTRL + Break** on your keyboard.

**38**

# 39

## Working with Security Settings

In this lesson, you will learn how to use security in Access 2007 using the Trust Center, encryption techniques and the new Package-and-Sign feature.

# → The Trust Center

The *Trust Center* is really just a dialogue box that you can use to set and change security settings, such as creating or changing trusted locations or establishing security options.

It contains logic for evaluating databases so, when the Trust Center senses danger, it will disable the content.

That's because, by default, Access simply disables any code or components that it views as being unsafe, then informs you of the action by displaying a message bar, as shown. When you see the message bar, you decide what to do – trust the database for the current session, trust it forever or continue with the disablement. It's pretty simple.

When you see the message bar, follow these steps to trust it for the *current session only*.

**1** Click on **Options**.

**2** Click on **Enable this content**, as shown in Figure 39.1.

**3** Click on **OK**.

To trust the database *permanently*, follow these steps.

**1** Click on **Options** in the message bar.

**2** Click on **Open the Trust Center** in the **Security Alert**.

**3** Click on **Trusted Locations** in the **Trust Center**, as shown.

**4** Click on **Add new location**.

**5** In the **Microsoft Office Trusted Locations dialogue box**, type the file path and folder name where you want the database to reside as a trusted location.

**Figure 39.1**
A security alert will appear when Access 2007 has disabled content in a database due to potentially unsafe content.

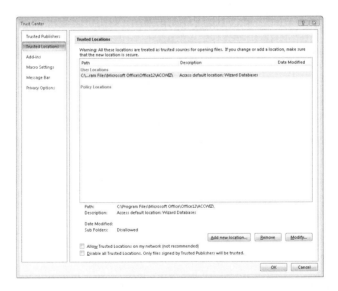

## Important

A trusted database must reside on a *local* drive, unless you have specifically allowed trusted network locations.

**6** Click on **OK**.

**7** Click on **OK** in the **Trust Center**.

To complete the process of trusting the database permanently, follow this next series of steps.

**1** In the database, click on the **Microsoft Office button**.

**2** Go to **Save As** and click on an available option under **Save the database in another format**.

**3** In the **Save As dialogue box**, locate and select the trusted location.

**4** Click on **Save**.

## → Adding or Removing a Developer from a Trusted Location

In Access, a *developer* is anyone who creates a macro, ActiveX control, add-in or another application extension within a database. *Trusted publishers* are reputable developers who meet the following criteria:

- the code project is signed with a digital signature by a trusted publisher

- the digital signature is valid as well as current

- the certificate for the digital signature is issued by a reputable certificate authority.

To add a developer to a trusted location, follow these steps.

**1** Open the **Security Alert**.

**2** Select **Trust all documents from this publisher**.

**3** Click on **OK**.

To remove a developer from a trusted location, follow these steps.

**1** Click on the **Microsoft Office button**.

**2** Click on **Access Options**.

**3** Click on **Trust Center**.

**4** Click on **Trust Center Settings**.

**5** Click on **Trusted Publishers**.

**6** Click on the name that you want to remove in the **Prior Trusted Sources list**.

**7** Click on **Remove**.

## → Changing a Trusted Location

If you need to change a trusted location, follow these steps.

**1** Click on the **Microsoft Office button**.

**2** Click on **Access Options**.

**3** Click on **Trust Center**.

**4** Click on **Trust Center Settings**.

**5** Click on **Trusted Locations**.

**6** Click on the trusted location under **Path** that you need to change, as shown.

**39**

| Path | Description | Date Modified |
|------|-------------|---------------|
| User Locations | | |
| C:\...ram Files\Microsoft Office\Office12\ACCWIZ\ | Access default location: Wizard Databases | |
| Policy Locations | | |

**7** Click on **Modify**.

**8** Click on **OK**.

**9** In the **Path box**, locate and select the folder that you want to use as the new trusted location, as shown.

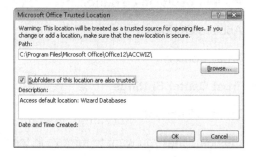

**10** Add subfolders as desired by selecting **Subfolders of this location are also trusted**.

**11** Type in the purpose of the trusted location in the **Description** box.

**12** Click on **OK**.

### Jargon buster

**Encryption** is probably the most effective way to achieve strong data security for the average user. Encrypted data is known as *cipher text* and must be deciphered in order to read it. To read an encrypted file, you must have a password.

## → Encrypting your Database

When you use encryption with Access 2007, your data essentially becomes unreadable to anyone without a password. To encrypt your database by using a password, follow these steps:

**1** Click on the **Microsoft Office button**.

**2** Click on **Open**.

**3** Browse to the file you want to open. Click on the file.

**4** Click on the down arrow on the **Open button**, as shown.

**5** Click on **Open Exclusive**.

**6** Go to the **Database Tools** tab and click on **Encrypt with Password** in the **Database Tools group**, as shown.

39

**7** In the **Set Database Password dialogue box**, type in the password you want to use. Enter it again into the **Verify box**. Click on **OK**.

>
>
> **Important**
>
> The new encryption feature is only available for .accdb files. It's a tougher encryption code than ever before to help you conceal information and prevent unauthorised use of your database.

## → Opening an Encrypted Database

If you need to decrypt your database, follow these steps.

**1** Open the encrypted database.

**2** Enter your password at the prompt.

> **Important**
>
> **If you forget your password for an encrypted database, there is no way that it can be retrieved**. To avoid losing it, write it down and keep it somewhere safe, but easily accessible.

## → Removing a Password from an Encrypted Database

If you decide that a password is no longer necessary for your database, follow these steps to remove it.

**1** Click on the **Microsoft Office button**.

**2** Click on **Open**.

**3** Browse to the file you want to open. Click on the file.

**4** Click on the down arrow on the **Open button**.

**5** Click on **Open Exclusive**.

**6** Go to the **Database Tools tab** and click on **Decrypt Database** in the **Database Tools group**.

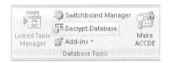

**7** In the **Unset Database Password dialogue box**, type in your password.

**8** Click on **OK**.

## → Using the Package-and-Sign Feature

When you create a database with the file extensions '.accdb' or '.accde', you can package the file, add a digital signature to it and distribute the signed package to others. Packaging and signing a database will make it easier for others to trust your database when it arrives. To use the Package-and-Sign feature, you must have at least one security certificate available.

39

To create a self-signed security certificate, follow these steps.

**1** In Microsoft Windows Vista, click on **Start**.

**2** Click on **All Programs**.

**3** Click on **Microsoft Office**.

**4** Click on **Microsoft Office Tools**.

**5** Click on **Digital Certificate for VBA Projects**, as shown.

**6** In the **Create Digital Certificate dialogue box**, type in the name for your certificate, as shown.

**7** Click on **OK**. The **SelfCert Success dialogue box** will appear, as shown.

**8** Click on **OK**.

To create a signed package, follow these steps.

**1** In the database you want to package and sign, click on the **Microsoft Office button**.

**2** Point to **Publish**. Click on **Package and Sign**.

**3** Select the certificate desired in the **Select Certificate dialogue box**. Click on **OK**.

**4** In the **Create Microsoft Office Access Signed Package**, find and select the location of the signed database package, as shown.

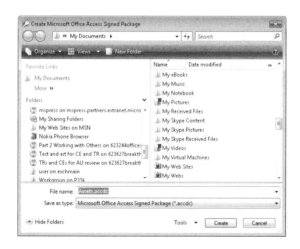

**5** Enter a name for the signed package in the **File Name box**.

**6** Click on **Create**. Access will create the .accdc file and put it in the location you selected.

**Important**

Only one database can be added to a package.